Praise for *Journeys in Long-Term Care*

"Michael Meulemans has turned decades of expertise into a practical guide for families facing their most difficult decisions. *Journeys in Long-Term Care* demystifies one of the most complex systems in American healthcare—and does so with clarity, compassion, and real-world wisdom."

— Joshua Boynton, Founder of LifeShare

"*Journeys in Long-Term Care* is a must-read for anyone facing the maze of long-term care. Michael Meulemans brings clarity, compassion, and deep expertise to one of the most confusing aspects of our healthcare system. Families, caregivers, and professionals alike will find practical guidance and real-world insight in every chapter."

— Todd Costello, Executive Director –
Community Living Alliance

"*Journeys in Long-Term Care* by Michael Meulemans is a very well organized and valuable resource for anyone trying to navigate the complicated world of Medicaid, Medicare and our Long-term Care system."

— Rob Gundermann, President – Coalition
of Wisconsin Aging Groups

Journeys in Long-Term Care

Michael Meulemans

CKBooks Publishing

The laws and regulations discussed in this book vary by state and jurisdiction and are subject to change. For specific guidance on these programs and rules consult an attorney, insurance professional, or your local Aging and Disability Resource Center.

The author has used his best efforts in the writing of this book but makes no representation or warranties as to its completeness or accuracy. All information herein was written and vetted by the author. Any advice given in this book is not guaranteed or warrantied and may not be suitable for every situation given the unique nuances of individual eligibility and long-term care needs and circumstances. Neither the author nor CKBooks Publishing shall be liable for any losses suffered by the reader of this book. Contact the author at www.theLTCResource.com.

Publisher's Cataloging-in-Publication Data
Names: Meulemans, Michael, 1969- .
Title: Journeys in long-term care : navigating our most complex health system / Michael Meulemans.
Description: New Glarus, WI : CKBooks Publishing, 2026. | Includes bibliographical references. | Summary: Helps readers understand long-term care options, Medicare, Medicaid, disability, and veterans' benefits, using examples of three people/families who have dealt with any one of these items, illustrating their struggles and things that were helpful.
Identifiers: LCCN 2026902922 | ISBN 9781966219217 (hardcover) | ISBN 9781966219200 (pbk) | ISBN 9781966219224 (ebook)
Subjects: LCSH: Medicare – Handbooks, manuals, etc. | Medicaid – Handbooks, manuals, etc. | Social security – Handbooks, manuals, etc. | Veterans – Medical care – Handbooks, manuals, etc. | Disability insurance – Handbooks, manuals, etc. | Long-term care insurance – Handbooks, manuals, etc. | Health insurance – Wisconsin. | BISAC: MEDICAL / Medicaid & Medicare. | MEDICAL / Long-Term Care. | FAMILY & RELATIONSHIPS / Eldercare.
Classification: LCC RA412.3 .M48 2026 | DDC 368.4/2--dc23
LC record available at https://lccn.loc.gov/2026902922

Cover design by Sadia Naeem

CKBooks Publishing
P.O. Box 214
New Glarus, WI 53574
www.ckbookspublishing.com

This book is dedicated to my parents, Don and Kate Meulemans. Their love and support for each other and their children have always been unconditional and an incredible example to my sisters and me. Their love and care for one another through 63 years of marriage grew stronger with each passing year. Throughout their lives they volunteered in their community and were a tremendous example of service and dedication to others.

My father and mother, Don and Kate in 2021.

Acknowledgments

This book would not be possible without the inspiration to write, research, and advocate what I learned from so many. First, I received my love of books from my late father, Don. His love of history and biographies led him to read voraciously, satisfying his curiosity about the world around him. He famously did not like to travel much to my mother's chagrin, but through his books he traveled afar, especially through the works of James A. Michener. Thanks Dad, for sharing your thirst for knowledge and books and countless other gifts, including your unending devotion to Mom, your work ethic, and dedicated community service.

Second, I'd like to acknowledge my late mother, Kate, through whom I learned faith and tireless devotion. Mom also provided the suggestion to take a job long ago in the health insurance industry and set me on this path, which has led to the completion of this book – a lifelong goal that is now in print. It's so meaningful that this work is centered on you and Dad and your dedication to each other.

To my sisters, Ann and Sue, for their love, partnership, and dedication in caring for our parents. You both inspire with everything you do for them and your love and support for me goes beyond words. Thanks for helping put our story on paper and sharing this journey. Because of you both, others can learn from our parents' story, as well as the stories of Cassie, Jay, and Aaron.

Of course, this book would not be possible without dedicated family members caring for their loved ones, like thousands of other people across this world. I am thankful for and want to acknowledge Bill, Lisa, and Lori for sharing their caregiver journeys with me. Thanks for your trust, patience, and putting up with my endless questions. I hope your love, care, and advocacy for Aaron, Cassie, and Jay leaps off the page.

I would like to thank Christine Keleny and CKBooks Publishing for exceptional support, editing, and consultation in finalizing and publishing this book. I so appreciate your guidance and expertise throughout the editing and publishing process.

Over the last few years, I have enjoyed my time and involvement on the Community Living Alliance and the Alzheimer's Association of Wisconsin Boards of Directors. I'd like to thank Todd Costello – Executive Director of Community Living Alliance – and its board of directors. I have enjoyed working with you all to improve services in southern Wisconsin for those who have disabilities and for elderly individuals. And thank you also to Dave Grams – Executive Director of the Alzheimer's Association of Wisconsin (AAW) and to its Board of Directors. The work you do to advance Alzheimer's research and dementia care, knowledge, and resources across Wisconsin makes a difference for tens of thousands of Wisconsin families every year, including mine. I have learned so much while a member of the AAW board as well and am inspired by your advocacy and service.

I would also like to acknowledge and especially thank two long-term colleagues whom I have worked with to advance Medicaid services, Paige Fleming and Jim Wojciechowski. It has been beyond amazing to work with such dedicated and committed writers each day striving to advance Medicaid and long-term care (LTC) services. Your expertise and commitment to the Medicaid cause is unmatched, except by your friendship. Likewise, I have received tremendous support and encouragement in this effort from other colleagues and friends including Josh Boynton, the Waypoint Guys, and many others. Thank you so much!

Lastly and most personally I want to acknowledge Mary Pearson. Your support, Mary, in completing this project has been unwavering at every turn. Your understanding and belief in both my day-to-day work and this book project means more to me than I can possibly put into words. Of course, you know I am rarely at a loss for words when it comes to sharing my passion for enhancing Medicaid and long-term care services. I love that you understand and share my passion for what I have made my life's work. Thanks for listening all those times and most of all, sharing this journey with me.

Table of Contents

Introduction

My goal with this book is to help make sense of the long-term care landscape facing those in need and their families so they can best manage their care. Through reviews of Medicare, Medicaid, and long-term care insurance and other insurance and benefit sources you will see where, how, and when coverage is attained. Readers will also find ways to navigate resources amid the incongruent puzzle of care, payment, and access. Although individual long-term care needs are unique, the four cases illustrated within these pages will serve to create better understanding of managing a loved one's needs and circumstances.

First, we will look at the health care landscape and how it impacts long-term care coverage and benefit access by reviewing long-term care insurance, Medicaid, Medicare, the Affordable Care Act, and veteran's services. Of the health insurance coverage types we'll discuss, only Medicaid, the VA, and long-term care insurance provide coverage for nursing-home-level care for those who are chronically ill or in the latter stages of life when they are compromised by incontinence, lack of mobility, and inability to properly care for themselves. My hope is that an overview of long-term care coverage, coupled with four specific long-term care journeys and their insights, will be beneficial and allay and demystify the complexity of long-term care.

Throughout my thirty-year career I have worked and focused on health care policy specifically related to long-term care services. As a result, ensuring and improving LTC services and access is very personal to me. I believe access to health coverage and benefits is a fundamental human right. Earlier in my career I worked in Medicaid policy for the Wisconsin

Department of Health Services for 12 years. During those 12 years, I worked alongside three dedicated policy professionals who had spinal cord injuries and accessed Medicaid-covered personal assistance services to support their employment. Together we worked to improve Medicaid benefits and work incentives for people with disabilities. Each of these individuals' lived experience and their daily perseverance was inspirational to me as a person without a physical disability. I learned through them how valuable Medicaid support and benefits are for leading a meaningful life and was inspired by how they worked every day as civil servants to improve the lives of Wisconsinites with disabilities.

For the last 14 years I have worked in the Medicaid managed care industry, helping to both improve access to and enhance Medicaid and long-term care coverage and benefits. In addition to these work experiences directly related to Medicaid coverage and policy and with these exceptional individuals I noted above, I also have relationships with family and others who rely on Medicaid coverage and services. Because of all this experience, I am first and foremost an advocate, in addition to being a long-term care policy and services expert. By no means do I have expertise in every aspect of Medicaid, but in my 25 years working in both the public and private sectors, I have gained expertise in long-term care issues concerning the aged and those with disabilities. I have also worked briefly in Medicare and consulted on the Affordable Care Act at the time of its implementation in 2013. So, I am well-versed in all aspects of government health coverage options and long-term care policy and benefits.

Every conversation I have with friends in our 40s and 50s inevitably turns to discussions about our parents and their health status, long-term care needs, and how they are managing their care. We are the sandwich generation. We have kids in college, high school, or perhaps younger who have tremendous needs, but we also spend a lot of time caring for our parents. Some of us are even direct caregivers for our parents. Many of us with parents who are still healthy and thriving often hear how they are worried about paying for the care they need as they age. Few have a plan, and fewer have long-term care insurance. Family caregivers have a critical role in caring for our kids and parents – at both ends of the age continuum. This balancing act can take a tremendous, frustrating toll.

The four journeys depicted include a wide variety of long-term care issues facing specific individuals including how their care is financed and how they and their family navigate access to care. The names of my journey subjects and members of their families depicted in journeys 2, 3, and 4 have been changed for privacy.

The first journey involves my elderly parents in their eighties residing in an assisted living facility with long-term care insurance coverage. The second journey is the story of a 52-year-old man who had a stroke mid-career and is seeking a Social Security disability approval and is hoping to continue working or volunteering in his community. The third journey focuses on a 53-year-old man with Down syndrome and developmental disabilities since birth. The fourth journey is centered on a young woman with autism who is legally blind, trying to gain Social Security disability benefits and Medicaid coverage.

As with these individuals, America's fragmented health system makes it extremely difficult for many to navigate and access coverage and benefits. We have dozens of ways Americans gain access to coverage for health-related illnesses and injuries. To make matters more complex, the means to access standard medical care for illnesses and injuries is completely different than accessing long-term care services. In the end what we have is the most complicated system of health care of any industrialized nation.

The US is by far the richest country without universal health care. And yet our health costs are also the highest per capita of any industrialized nation, often double or triple those of other nations. In 2023 the US spent an exorbitant portion of our Gross Domestic Product, 17.6%[1] for health care expenditures, but it has been higher. During the COVID-19 pandemic, health care expenditures actually dropped dramatically due to under-utilization. Three years earlier, in 2020, health care expenditures were 19.7% of GDP.

There is no question in my mind that when we get the 2024 GDP numbers, it will, unfortunately, have rebounded to new heights as we once again access care at "normal" levels. Health care expenditures have risen dramatically over the last two decades in the US; health care expenditures as part of GDP were just 8.9% in 1980 and 13.3% in 2000.[2] In fiscal year 2023, almost $112.8 billion (or 12.8%) was spent on home- and community-based long-term-care services, while another $60.4 billion (or 6.8%) went for institutional long-term care. All told, 19.6% of all Medicaid spending went to long-term care.[3]

So what benefit has the US garnered with these exorbitant health care costs? Have we gained dramatically improved health outcomes in comparison to countries like Norway, Australia, and others? According to a report in 2024 by the Commonwealth Fund, the US ranked last among the top ten industrialized nations in overall health care rankings. The US was ranked tenth specifically in the areas of access to care and health outcomes.[4] This report compares health care system performance in Australia, Canada, France, Germany, the Netherlands, New Zealand, Norway, Sweden, Switzerland, the United Kingdom, and the United States. The report found the top-performing countries overall are Australia, the Netherlands, and the United Kingdom. In 2024, according to the Institute for Health Metrics, America ranked 50th in terms of lifespan and 68th in the world in terms of health span.[5] Health span focuses on the quality of those years lived, emphasizing vitality, independence, and physical and mental well-being. That same report also notes that the US ranks last on access to care, administrative efficiency, equity, and health care outcomes, but second on measures of care process (a consistently implemented set of methods and procedures). So, we have the care processes of a successful health system but fail miserably on care access, efficiency, and outcomes. This book will show why the fragmented, inefficient system we have creates barriers in accessing long-term care and where the cracks are that families need to be aware of. I have seen this access to care difficulty in my dad's wait in 2025 for a neurology consult when our family and the assisted living staff became concerned about possible dementia.

Breakdown of US Health Coverage by Insurance and Government Program Type

Total US Individuals Insured	304 (92.1%)*
Private Health Insurance—Employer-based	180 (54.7%)
Private Health Insurance—Individual/Direct-Purchase	46 (13.9%)
Medicaid/CHIP	70 (21.3%)
Medicare	62 (18.8%)
Military—TRICARE	9 (2.8%)
Military—VA Care	7 (2.2%)
Uninsured	26 (7.9%)

Key – numbers in millions, *7.9% of US population is uninsured

His primary care physician referred him for the neurology consult in early January. We were told it was a six-eight month wait, and we would be called in four-five months to schedule the appointment. This is a pervasive concern as, "four in five older adults (82%) say the US health care system is not prepared for the growing and changing needs of America's aging population. Just 1 in 10 [Americans] (11%) give the health care system an 'A' grade."[6]

Many Americans are concerned a move to nationalized health care like that which exists in Canada or England would include rationing of care. We already have rationed care with these types of long waits to gain access to needed appointments. Nearly three of five (57%) underinsured adults said they avoided getting needed health care because of its cost; 44% of consumers said they had medical or dental debt they were paying off over time. Delaying care has health consequences: two of five (41%) working-age adults who reported a cost-related delay in their care said a health problem had worsened because of it.[7]

The focus of my effort in this book is to help individuals and families understand how various insurance types provide access to long-term care coverage. To do this we first need a thorough overview of the complexity that is the American health care coverage system and how long-term care coverage is left on the sidelines. This book's focus is not about health care reform, but I cannot ignore the underlying facts of how our government programs have been set up to fail those in need. By not having a comprehensive, universal entry point to access and navigate an incredibly complex system of care, Americans are largely on their own to access the means to gain health coverage. While our government leaders at every level struggle to improve our health care system with new programs, regulations, and health care provider requirements, the system becomes more complex for citizens to access the care they need. As a result, the health care system and means to access coverage is unnecessarily confusing. It's akin to putting together a complex jigsaw puzzle with both missing pieces and pieces that simply do not fit.

While the complexity of America's health care and insurance system makes it very difficult to navigate, it's also important to realize every individual has their own unique health care needs and obstacles to care. While each individual story has its unique attributes, including the four stories in this book, we can learn from other's paths and resources used to navigate the care we each need.

Many people I talk to about the American health insurance landscape are confused and frustrated by its complexity. It is so complex that many Americans put off planning and considering how to address their care needs. They may be too focused on raising children and work and then planning for retirement that they neglect to plan what their later retirement years will look like. "It gets late, early" is a phrase I have come to think of over and over while writing this book. That famous malaprop uttered by the great Yankee catcher, Yogi Berra, was about late afternoon shadows during day games at Yankee Stadium. But it is also the best phrase I can think of when discussing with folks the need for long-term care planning. Failing to plan for long-term care needs will cause it to get late earlier than people think, and they will often be unprepared when the time comes.

> "It gets late, early."
>
> Yogi Berra,
> New York Yankee Hall of Famer and Philosopher

I believe many fail to make long-term care plans effectively in large part because the system is so challenging and complex. For instance, many individuals do not know the specifics of how Medicaid coverage is accessed or how many individuals are covered by it. The same is true as many Americans are confused about how Medicare and Medicare Advantage plans interrelate and the extent to which they cover long-term care needs. This book attempts to provide an understanding of the important nuances related to long-term care services, to dispel frustration and confusion, and demystifying Medicaid, Medicare, veteran's benefits and the components of our most complex health system.

PART I

Overview of American Insurance Resources

Chapter I

Long-Term Care Insurance

As we came into this world as infants, every single one of us required long-term care (LTC) services. As infants we are completely helpless and dependent upon others for every need and activity of daily living – feeding, bathing, dressing, transferring, and more. The majority of us will unfortunately return to having those everyday essential needs fulfilled by others. As with our infancy, it is almost as inescapable. Yet, few individuals deliberately plan for the provision of their long-term care needs.

So how do we meet those needs – through loved ones or outside caretakers? Many of us in our later years do not have spouses, children, or other family members ready and able to provide care. In those instances, financing the costs of LTC in either a nursing home or assisted living facility is an expensive proposition. Only a small portion of American seniors have long-term care insurance. As of 2020, according to the American Association for Long-Term Care Insurance, only 7% of US adults over the age of 50 have a long-term care insurance policy.[8]

Over the next ten years, the number of residents in LTC facilities is expected to grow sharply. If trends hold up, the number of nursing home residents could increase by over

75% to 2.3 million residents by 2030, according to Consumer Affairs Journal. It is estimated that in 2030 a semi-private nursing home room will cost more than $10,400 per month.[9] These changes are due to multiple factors, including our aging population and declining numbers of available care staff. The effects of the caregiver shortage will only exacerbate costs and will likely reduce the quality of care.

Future Prognosis for Long-Term Care Needs and Insurance

Given the projected increase in need described above, there will be enormous pressure on the care system expected while the number of care providers diminishes. The baby boomers will "put enormous pressure on the care system, not only because there are so many in that generation but because they are living longer," Bryan Langdon, Ash Brokerage's national spokesperson for long-term care said during a speech at the National Association of Insurance and Financial Advisors' Peak 65 Impact Day.[10] If the supply of care in the form of long-term care facilities or home care workers doesn't accelerate to keep up with demand, the price of receiving care will skyrocket, Langdon continued.

Robert Eaton of Milliman, Inc., a Medicaid actuary firm, pointed to LTC claims stemming from Alzheimer's disease and other forms of dementia as driving the cost and duration of care. "Cognitive impairment claims make up 40% of all claims paid by long-term care insurers." Medical advancements are enabling doctors to diagnose dementia and Alzheimer's sooner and "We're finding that people are living more healthily earlier in life but then have a longer long-term care need,"[11] he said.

Long-term care insurance typically provides coverage for home health services, assisted living centers, nursing home services, memory care facility services, adult day care, and hospice. But not all long-term care insurance plans cover the entirety of those facility and benefit types.

Long-term care insurance policy provisions and requirements

Activities of Daily Living (ADL):

Everyday functions and activities individuals usually do without help. ADLs include bathing, continence, dressing, feeding, toileting, and transferring. Many policies determine benefit eligibility based on being unable to do two of six ADLs.

Adult Daycare:

Care given during the day at a community-based center for adults who need help or supervision. This includes help with daily personal care but does not include around-the-clock care.

Assisted Living Facility:

A residential living arrangement that provides personal care and health services. Assisted living is for people who need assistance with activities of daily living, but don't need the level of care a nursing home provides. These facilities can range from small homes to large apartment-style complexes and may offer different levels of care and services.

Benefit Triggers:

The criteria an insurer uses to decide when a policy pays benefits. This often includes being unable to do two or more activities of daily living or needing substantial supervision due to cognitive impairment such as dementia or Alzheimer's.

Cognitive Impairment:

A loss of short- or long-term memory; difficulty knowing people, places, or the time or season; loss of the ability to make good decisions; or loss of safety awareness.

Daily Maximum Benefit:

The amount the policy will pay for each day of care, often limited to the amount charged for the care.

Elimination Period:

The "elimination period" is the amount of time that must pass after a benefit trigger occurs but before receipt of payment for services. An elimination period is like the deductible an insured pays on car insurance, except it is measured in time rather than by dollar amount.

Hands-On Assistance:

Physical help (minimal, moderate, or maximal) an individual needs to do an activity of daily living.

Home Health Care:

Care services received in the home. It can include nursing care, social services, medical care, homemaker services, and occupational, physical, respiratory, or speech therapy.

Inflation Protection Rider:

A policy option that provides for increases in benefit levels to help pay for expected increases in the costs of long-term care services. Annual increases are based on inflation and are adjusted each year the policy is in force.

Maximum Lifetime Benefit:

The approximate number of years a policyholder wants the

policy to provide benefits will determine the Maximum Lifetime Benefit. The longer the period of coverage, the higher the premium. The lifetime maximum benefit is computed by multiplying the Daily Maximum benefit selected by the approximate number of days the insured wants benefits to be paid or reimbursed.

Memory Care:

A memory care facility is a long-term care residence, or nursing home. Memory care is designed to help individuals with cognitive decline or other memory issues such as dementia or Alzheimer's Disease. Memory care can happen in many different settings.

Partnership Policy:

A type of LTC policy that lets you protect (keep) some of your assets if you apply for Medicaid after you exhaust your LTC policy's benefits. Partnership policies may not be available in all states.

Spend Down:

A requirement where an individual must spend most of his or her income and assets to meet Medicaid eligibility requirements.

Stand-by Assistance:

When a caregiver stays close to watch a person and offer physical help if needed.

Waiver of Premium:

An insurance policy feature that allows an insured who is receiving benefits to no longer pay premiums.

Long-Term Care Public-Private Partnership Policies

As of December 2024, every state except Hawaii, Alaska, Utah, and Mississippi, as well as Washington, D.C., have a version of LTC insurance policies called Partnership policies. The term Partnership relates to how the policies create a partnership between long-term care insurance and Medicaid coverage of long-term care services. As an example: If the Partnership policy paid $200,000, Medicaid would allow a policyholder to keep $200,000 in assets and then still qualify for government help to pay for care as long as individuals meet all other qualifications. Long-term care partnership policies must include inflation protection coverage that meets specific minimum standards based on your age at the time you apply for a qualified long-term care partnership policy. Like other long-term care insurance policies, Partnership policy benefits are based on daily reimbursement maximums (e.g., $170/ day for nursing home coverage). Eligibility rules concerning the purchase of "Partnership" policies at age intervals related to inflation protection provisions include the following:

- Applicants purchasing policies must be under age 61 when they buy the policy. It will provide annual compounded inflation increases for benefits to cover the cost of care.
- For applicants between age 61 and 76, the policy will provide simple inflation increases for covered benefits in alignment with inflation increases as it occurs in the general economy.
- For applicants over age 76, the policy might or might not provide inflation increases.

All long-term care partnership policies are intended to be federally tax-qualified long-term care insurance policies as defined by federal Internal Revenue code.

LTC Insurance Coverage Types:

Home Health Care

Home health care is covered by both Medicare Part A and B (depending on individual circumstances) and under long-term care insurance. Medicare typically covers skilled home health services, like care from a registered nurse and/or a speech, physical, or occupational therapist. However, it does not cover what's called home care services, also known as custodial home care or personal care (daily, basic, non-medical care, like eating and bathing). In some cases, Medicare will send a home health aide to assist with bathing and dressing, but the hours and duration are typically extremely limited, and you may not be able to choose the home care agency. In contrast, most long-term care insurance policies cover home health services, including a wide range of needs: homemaking and companionship to meal preparation and medication reminders. Home care may also include personal care services, or those that help with the activities of daily living, including home care services like bathing, dressing, and grooming. To promote a safe and functional lifestyle, a caregiver can help you brush your teeth, secure the buttons on your shirt, or stand by while individuals bathe to make sure they do not slip or fall.

Often, skilled services that utilize the expertise of a nurse may also be grouped within the home care category. Services include checking vital signs, coordinating with doctors and other health care professionals working with the individual, and performing comprehensive evaluations of health and community needs to keep individuals safe at home.

For those that cannot afford a private home health care aid, they often resort to the use of family caregivers. A 2020 report by the National Alliance for Caregiving and AARP estimated that one in five of the estimated 53 million caregivers in this country care for an adult. That adult is often a family member providing unpaid care. Many of those caregivers remain in the traditional workforce while balancing that care for their loved one.[12] These circumstances hit minority groups harder as Hispanic and African American caregivers devote more hours to caregiving, according to the study. Specifically, nearly 50% of Hispanic caregivers are more often in a high-intensity care situation than non-Hispanic white and Asian caregivers and on average provide care for 26 hours a week.

Assisted Living Facilities

An assisted living facility is a residential apartment-based community for older adults. It allows residents to remain independent in their own private living unit, but with available assistance for activities of daily living and 24/7 support services. People in an assisted living community don't need intensive medical care that is provided in a nursing home, but they may need help and support with essential daily activities like medication management. Assisted living facilities often offer social activities, offsite shopping trips, fitness programs, and on-site podiatry care and salon services.

Nursing Home Care

Coverage in nursing homes is included in the vast majority of LTC policies. Most long-term care insurance policies provide payment for what's commonly called "activities of daily living" (ADL). It covers the cost of residency in a nursing home facility, medical attention, medications, daily assistance with hygiene, meals, and daily social or "quality of life" activities for nursing home residents. In general, this coverage applies to:

- Room and board

- Skilled nursing care
- Help with personal care
- Therapies as needed

Adult Day Care

Coverage of adult day care services is often available at a stand-alone facility during the day at a community-based center for adults. The program includes supervision and daily personal care and a range of benefits, including socialization, health monitoring, and rehabilitation services, providing a safe and engaging environment during daytime hours. Adult day care services have emerged as an important solution for families who care for their loved ones' long-term care needs. These caregivers are often balancing their own growing families, jobs, and are seeking support and respite in caring for their elderly or disabled loved ones. For many caregivers, adult day care centers serve as a lifeline, offering respite care and peace of mind while allowing their family members to maintain independence and quality of life.

Adult Family Home (AFH)

An AFH is the smallest type of residential facility. Often a private home can contain one to four residents, along with caregivers who may or may not live there. Residents receive care "above the level of room and board," which can include up to seven hours per week of nursing care. Most AFHs specialize in a particular type of resident such as those with Down syndrome. In Wisconsin AFHs of one and two beds are controlled by the local county or managed care organization, while three and four bed AFHs are regulated by the state of Wisconsin Division of Quality Assurance (DQA).

Community-Based Residential Facility (CBRF)

The Wisconsin State Legislature has defined CBRFs as giving care to people who "do not require care above intermediate level nursing care" and require no more than three hours of care per week. The primary difference between a CBRF and a nursing home is that while residents of both receive nursing care, those in nursing homes require care above "intermediate level nursing care" and of more than three hours of care per week. Those individuals residing in CBRFs are thus relatively independent versus those in nursing homes and in many cases those in assisted living facilities. The term CBRF is not used in all states and guidelines on levels of care in long-term care facilities differ as well. For information on unique state requirements visit your state's Department of Health Services website or similar agency.

Memory Care

Memory care refers to a set of services tailored for people with dementia and or Alzheimer's disease. These services are provided by trained staff who aim to help patients safely maintain their independence and a good quality of life. Memory-focused care can be provided in nursing homes, assisted living communities, specialized memory care facilities, or even at a person's home. Memory care facilities focus on reducing isolation through specialized cognitive activities.

Memory care facilities also focus on providing a safe and structured environment with set routines to reduce stress for residents with memory issues. Key features of memory care include the key components of assisted and nursing home care but also include:

- **Specialized Staff Training:** Staff members receive training in handling specific memory-related conditions and behaviors, allowing them to provide tailored care.

- **Secure Environment:** Facilities are designed to prevent wandering, a common issue for those with memory disorders, ensuring residents are safe. Memory care facilities also allow retention of some independence but provide their clients a safeguarded environment.
- **Therapeutic Activities:** Structured activities encourage cognitive function and reduce anxiety, including music therapy, art activities, and memory games.
- **Personalized Care Plans:** Residents receive care based on their specific needs, with plans frequently updated as conditions change.

At the time of this writing, 37 states have regulations that define "memory care" and mandate training requirements for memory care staff in long-term care facilities. Wisconsin does not currently have such requirements though legislation is being considered in the Wisconsin legislature during the 2025-2026 legislative session. For now, Wisconsin long-term care facilities can label and market themselves as providing memory care services without defined or enforced standards.

CHAPTER II

Employer-Based Insurance Coverage

Many Americans think employer-based health insurance covers the vast majority of Americans. In fact, traditional employer-based health insurance covers only about 54% of the US population as of December 2023.[13] Most employers offer health insurance coverage, but that coverage does not include long-term care services within its benefit structure. Some employers offer long-term care coverage as a supplemental insurance coverage similar to dental insurance or disability insurance.

Employer-offered disability insurance does not pay for care or services. Instead, short or long-term disability insurance pays part of an employee's income if they are too sick or out of work for an extended period due to an injury or illness. Disability insurance may cover 50% to 80% of your salary, depending on various factors. There are two main types of disability insurance: short-term and long-term. Short-term coverage typically pays benefits for three to six months, although some policies extend up to a year. The waiting period before benefits begin is usually 14 to 30 days, but some policies offer shorter delays before coverage begins. Long-term disability coverage offers income support for extended periods, helping with income replacement during prolonged illness or life-changing injuries. Long-term disability coverage can extend several years or until retirement, during serious health issues. Illustrated in the second journey, Jay's story involves his mid-career stroke, where his employer-based coverage plays an important role, particularly his long-term disability coverage. Over 35% of employers offer disability insurance coverage to their employees in some shape or form, according to data from the Bureau of Labor Statistics.[14]

Chapter III

Affordable Care Act / ObamaCare

The Patient Protection and Affordable Care Act (aka the ACA or ObamaCare) was signed into law by President Obama on March 23, 2010. The ACA significantly changed the health insurance system in the US by expanding coverage to many previously uninsured individuals. The ACA is a vital component of the US health care puzzle and thus why it is discussed at length in this book. It is also a key program related to Medicaid because of ACA provisions that extended coverage to fill care gaps for lower income Americans. All of this is very important for our consideration here even though the ACA does not include coverage of long-term care needs.

The Trump Administration in 2025 sought cost savings in administering the ACA in part by reducing the annual enrollment period by one month. The Federal Marketplace open enrollment period beginning for the 2027 plan year will run from November 1 through December 15. Coverage for enrollments during the open enrollment period must begin on January 1.[15] The State-run ACA Marketplaces where individuals purchase ACA policies have different enrollment periods. But those who lose health insurance coverage, have a qualifying life change, or have very low incomes can obtain policies throughout the year through special enrollment periods.

A Commonwealth Fund analysis found that the Affordable Care Act not only helped reduce the number of uninsured people in the US by almost 50%.[16] it also helped narrow racial and ethnic gaps in health care access and coverage, especially in states that expanded Medicaid eligibility. Progress continued during the pandemic, when over 5 million individuals gained health care coverage and the nationwide uninsured rate fell to 8%, but those gains could be reversed with the end of the public health emergency and the return of Medicaid eligibility redetermination, according to the report.

The ACA Expansion of Medicaid for Lower-Income Persons

The ACA Medicaid expansion extended Medicaid coverage to nearly all adults with incomes up to 138% of the Federal Poverty Level (FPL) (see Appendix I for a table of 2025 federal poverty guide-lines). In 2025, 138% of FPL is $21,597 for an individual and $44,367 for a family of four.[17] The ACA's Medicaid expansion provided states with an enhanced federal matching rate (FMAP) of 90% rather than the previous match of 80% for their expansion populations. In 2023 an estimated 26 million Americans, or 8% of the US population, lacked health insurance.[18] This is down from 49 million, or 16% of the population, who lacked health coverage prior to the ACA being enacted.[19] To date, 41 states (including DC) have adopted the Medicaid expansion and ten states, including Wisconsin, have not adopted the expansion. In states without Medicaid expansion, millions fall into a "coverage gap," earning too much to qualify for Medicaid but too little to qualify for Marketplace subsidies. It is estimated that roughly 1.5 million uninsured adults live in states that have not yet implemented the ACA Medicaid expansion.[20] In 2022 25.6 million nonelderly people remained uninsured in 2022, and six in ten of the uninsured people are eligible for Medicaid (6.4 million or 25%) or subsidized plans (35%) in the Marketplace but are not enrolled in these programs.[21] Among the remaining uninsured, 6% fall into the "coverage gap" because they live in one of the ten states that have not adopted the Medicaid expansion.

In the fall of 2025, the federal government shutdown due to the failure to pass an appropriations bill that would have funded the government through late November. Democrats in Congress refused to sign on unless changes were made to certain health care policies, including restoring Medicaid cuts enacted earlier in the year within the One Big Beautiful Bill Act (OBBBA) and retain subsidies provided by the ACA.

The ACA uses several means to achieve wider health insurance coverage for Americans. Through the ACA, private health insurance is offered via online marketplaces, often with a very substantial federal subsidy to pay the premiums. Subsidies are available to reduce insurance premiums for individuals in lower income brackets. Subsidies for higher income ACA enrollees extended by the Inflation Reduction Act (IRA) sunset at the close of 2025. They have not yet been extended and will result in higher premiums for those enrollees in 2026 if they are not extended.

The ACA reduced the amount individuals and families pay in uncompensated care by mandating coverage of ten essential benefit areas. The main goal of the ACA was to ensure that every American could afford a health insurance plan. This allowed families whose income put them at poverty level to be able to afford their health insurance premium through tax credits that were later upheld as lawful by the US Supreme Court.

ACA Essential Benefit Coverage

The reform law encouraged states to expand their Medicaid programs to cover more low-income people, and about half of the states have done so. The ACA requires health insurers to pay for basic services within ten essential benefit categories. As you'll see, the following list does not include long-term care services:

1. Ambulatory patient services (outpatient care you get without being admitted to a hospital)
2. Emergency services
3. Hospitalization (like surgery and overnight stays)
4. Pregnancy, maternity, and newborn care (both before and after birth)
5. Mental health and substance use disorder services, including behavioral health treatment (this includes counseling and psychotherapy)
6. Prescription drugs
7. Rehabilitative and habilitative services and devices (services and devices to help people with injuries, disabilities, or chronic conditions gain or recover mental and physical skills). This does not include long-term care services.
8. Laboratory services
9. Preventive and wellness services and chronic disease management
10. Pediatric services, including oral and vision care (but adult dental and vision coverage aren't essential health benefits)

The services covered do not vary by your location or which state an individual resides. However, some states require insurers to cover additional services and procedures.

Even within the same state, there can be small differences. When individuals compare plans in the Marketplace, they will see the specific benefits each plan offers.

The ACA imposes strict rules on health insurers that forbid them to drop sick, expensive clients and require them to accept even people with pre-existing conditions. With the 2024 Trump administration, it remains to be seen what changes may be made to the ACA as Donald Trump has long sought to repeal the law. During the 2024 campaign for the White House, he indicated he had "concepts of a plan," but he has not offered more details at the date this book is being published. Possible changes to the ACA and its Medicaid expansion provision include: imposing a per capita cap on federal Medicaid spending, reducing the federal government's share of costs for the ACA expansion group, imposing Medicaid work requirements, and possibly reducing the minimum federal matching rate for Medicaid expenditures, among others.[22] Dramatic policy changes like these would transform how Medicaid financing works, and federal spending reductions of this level would put states at severe financial risk, likely forcing them to slash the number of people covered, cover fewer benefits, and cut payment rates for physicians, hospitals, and nursing homes. The ripple effects would be enormous on hospitals, where there have been a rash of rural hospital closures in the last decade, and to nursing homes and other long-term care facilities.

Community Living Assistance Services and Supports, and Long-Term Care Provision Removed Before ACA Became Law

I risk obfuscating the information herein about long-term

care resources by bringing in politics, but unfortunately, they are intertwined to an extent that cannot be understated. Pulling on one health care policy lever and changing eligibility or financing impacts numerous others. All of the above elements of ACA coverage aid the broader health insurance market, but a void exists in addressing long-term care needs. While in the development stage prior to its passage into law, the ACA included a special provision, the Community Living Assistance Services and Supports Act (CLASS Act) to aid coverage of long-term care services. CLASS included components to address prevailing deficiencies in LTC financing through a national voluntary LTC insurance program administered by the Federal government. This component of the legislation was eliminated prior to its passage and was intended to supplement rather than supplant assistance received from other payers. CLASS relied on a cash benefit allocated by beneficiaries with the assistance of counseling services and included a consumer-directed philosophy. The provision was axed in part because it was felt there would be inadequate usage, particularly among healthier individuals with minimal long-term risks. Policymakers felt because of likely limited interest among the healthy, that CLASS would not fundamentally alter the existing public-private partnership for LTC financing. Instead, it was assumed that voluntary enrollment combined with a lack of medical underwriting would lead to higher enrollment among chronically ill individuals. Thus, it was eliminated from the ACA.

The ACA also included important provisions to aid those over age 65 as they advance in age and see increasing need for long-term care. Some of these provisions were in place within the original ACA legislation and some were added more recently. The following table identifies those elements that improved health care for seniors.

ACA Elements That Improve Care for Seniors

Original ACA Coverage Provisions

- The ACA's 2014 Medicaid expansion led to seniors being 4% more likely to have dual Medicare and Medicaid coverage, allowing for more affordable health care and better health outcomes and access to long-term care coverage through Medicaid
- Protection of care for pre-existing conditions for 32 million older Americans aged 55-64
- Seniors saved thousands on prescription drug costs. From 2010 to 2016, more than 11.8 million Medicare beneficiaries have received discounts over $26.8 billion on prescription drugs – an average of $2,272 per beneficiary
- Ensures that the more than 50 million people enrolled in Part D coverage (drug coverage) who may have otherwise fallen into a prescription drug coverage gap "donut hole" have their vital medications covered
- Guarantees no-cost coverage of preventive services, which has led to an increase in utilization among seniors and a decrease in catastrophic health costs
- Limited the amount older people could be charged to three times more than younger people. Previous to the ACA insurers were allowed much greater age-related premium differences

Improvements For Seniors on the ACA Since Its Passage

The 2020 Inflation Reduction Act:
- Lowered annual premiums for people who buy their own

coverage by an average of $2,400 per family, which has saved the average 60-year-old couple with a household income of $75,000 approximately $1,900 in monthly premiums for ACA coverage.
- Reduces out-of-pocket drug costs for Medicare enrollees by capping monthly insulin costs at $35, providing recommended vaccines at no cost, introducing a new annual out-of-pocket spending cap, and negotiating lower drug prices.
- Lower drug prices, including the new out-of-pocket cap on drug costs that went into effect in January 2024 and drops to $2,000 the out-of-pocket cap in 2025, which will save nearly 19 million seniors about $400 per year.

Some states have implemented the Basic Health Program to provide continuous coverage for low-income individuals whose income fluctuates above and below Medicaid eligibility. Through the Basic Health Program – an additional provision allowed by the ACA – states can provide coverage to individuals who are citizens or lawfully present non-citizens, who do not qualify for Medicaid, Children's Health Insurance Program (CHIP), or other minimum essential coverage and have income between 133% and 200% of the federal poverty level (FPL). Individuals who are lawfully present non-citizens who have income that does not exceed 133% of FPL but who are unable to qualify for Medicaid due to such non-citizen status, are also eligible to enroll as of this writing.

Enrolled individuals also benefit from the ten essential health benefits specified in the ACA. The monthly premium and cost sharing charged to eligible individuals will not exceed what an eligible individual would have paid if he or she were to receive coverage from a qualified health plan (QHP) through the ACA Marketplace. A state that operates a Basic

Health Program will receive federal funding equal to 95% of the amount of the premium tax credits and the cost sharing reductions that would have otherwise been provided to (or on behalf of) eligible individuals if these individuals enrolled in QHPs through the ACA Marketplace.

Minnesota implemented its Basic Health Program under the ACA on January 1, 2015. Oregon implemented theirs in 2024. New York had implemented a Basic Health Program in 2015 and suspended its program April 1, 2024.

ACA Subsidies and Tax Implications

Through 2025, the ACA provides subsidies for health insurance coverage for individuals making up to 400% of the Federal Poverty Level (FPL). For the first time, subsidies became available to those with income above four times the federal poverty level (FPL).[23] For those making more than the 400% threshold, if they purchase ACA coverage through the ACA Marketplace, they will pay no more than 8.5% of their household income for the benchmark silver plan. Subsidies help people pay their health insurance costs. One of these health insurance subsidies is the premium tax credit, which helps pay the monthly health insurance premiums. Premium subsidies are available in the ACA Market-place in every state. The American Rescue Plan made the subsidies larger and more widely available for 2021 and 2022 and became available for people at every income level. And the Inflation Reduction Act extended those subsidy enhancements through 2025.

Most individuals who enroll in ACA plans through the Marketplaces qualify for subsidies. As of early 2023, there were about 15.7 million people enrolled in health plans through the ACA Marketplaces nationwide, and about 14.3 million of them were receiving premium subsidies.[24]

To review and select ACA health plan options, go to

health care.gov. To learn more from a non-government source, go to health care.com. Many states set up their own marketplaces, but those states that did not, provide ACA health option at health care.gov.

The law was challenged almost as soon as it was passed, and its main provisions were on hold while the Supreme Court decided if it was even constitutional. In a landmark 2012 ruling, the court ruled that the law's individual mandate, requiring everyone to have health insurance or pay a fine, was constitutional. Chief Justice John Roberts wrote a compromise, calling the fine a tax, which made it legal. But the court said that states could choose whether to expand Medicaid. The law would have required them to do so. This is why the fine is seen as a tax and individuals with ACA coverage must ensure they adhere to ACA tax requirements when they file their annual income taxes. Consulting with a tax professional will help ensure compliance with the ACA-related tax provisions. This is important for those enrolling in the ACA to understand there are tax implications.

The ACA centered on creating affordability, medical care that is innovative, and the expansion of Medicaid. The expansion of Medicaid means that people who weren't previously eligible for the plan were eligible after the law was passed. See the chapter on Medicaid for information on its expansion with the enactment of the ACA.

ACA's Current Enrollment

Enrollment in the ACA has steadily increased over time even as there have been numerous attempts to debunk its worth to the millions who have enrolled in its coverage. Repeated efforts attempting to repeal the law have been thwarted, with the last attempts occurring in 2019. Enrollment for the 2025 plan year nationwide increased to an all-time record for ACA

Marketplace enrollment, with nearly 24 million Americans signing up for coverage with one week left in the 2025 Open Enrollment Period. A total of 45 million Americans have coverage through the ACA – either through the ACA Marketplace or Medicaid expansion,[25] a significant increase from 12.6 million in 2014, the year the coverage took effect. Since then, there has been an increase in the number of people who have become eligible for free or subsidized health care. This data includes the number of ACA enrollments in the Marketplace, Medicaid, and the Basic Health Program (BHP).

Enrollment in the ACA's health insurance marketplace at health care.gov have skyrocketed nearly 50% since the Biden administration took office in 2021. This dramatic increase is due largely to enhanced federal premium subsidies and increased outreach efforts. Plan selections are up 13% from 2024 to 2025.[26] The increase in coverage under the ACA resulted in reducing the US uninsured rate to an all-time low of 8% in the first quarter of 2022. For 2023, approximately 3.6 million people, or 22%, were new to ACA coverage, while the rest were existing enrollees who picked 2023 policies or were automatically reenrolled as existing enrollees.

Enrollees pay no more than 8.5% of their income toward coverage, down from nearly 10% prior to the enhancement legislated due to COVID-19, allowing more Americans to gain access to affordable coverage. Lower-income policyholders can receive subsidies that eliminate their premiums. Also, and as already mentioned, those earning more than 400% of the federal poverty level are now eligible for help. The new assistance allows about 80% of enrollees to find plans that cost less than $10 a month and has resulted in savings for enrollees of $800 a year on average in premiums last year, according to the federal Centers for Medicare and Medicaid Services.

Also, more families are eligible for subsidies on the ACA Marketplaces this year after the Biden administration finalized a rule addressing the "family glitch." The rule allows family members of workers who are offered affordable single coverage but unaffordable family policies to qualify for subsidies on the ACA Marketplaces for the first time.

Changes to the ACA Moving Forward

In 2025 the Trump administration made plans to save billions in administration of ACA Marketplace plans. Among new requirements, consumers would have to provide more information proving their eligibility for special enrollment periods and for premium subsidies when they enroll, eliminating some fraudulent enrollments. The regulation would also shorten the annual enrollment period by a month. This may also reduce enrollment numbers and create higher rates of uninsured, increasing amounts of uncompensated care for hospitals and other providers placing a strain on the safety net. Ultimately, increases in uncompensated care and the number of uninsured creates access problems for all and exacerbates the fragmentation in long-term care services.

For 2026 plan year, the Trump administration's proposals would eliminate the year-round opportunity for a special enrollment period for people with very low incomes. But it would also set new requirements for the remaining special enrollment periods, which allow people to sign up after major life events, such as when their income changes, they lose their job-based coverage, or they get divorced, marry, or move. New rules will likely also require additional paperwork and other eligibility requirements "will probably have a downward effect on enrollment," said Cynthia Cox, a vice president and the director of the Program on the ACA at KFF, a health information nonprofit that includes KFF Health News. "Some of that could be protecting enrollees who were fraudulently signed up or don't realize they're still signed up."[27]

As of January 2026, the enhanced tax credits reducing ACA plan costs for millions of Americans have expired. Congress failed to extend the tax credits even after a 43-day government shutdown forced by Democrats over the issue. Alternatives have not gained traction necessary to become law. The subsidies expiration caused premiums to spike, in some cases by more than 100 percent as the enrollment deadline neared in mid-January and solution is unlikely to be achieved.

Chapter IV

Medicaid

Medicaid is, I believe, the best and most cost-efficient component of America's horribly fragmented and dysfunctional health care system. As of January 2025, 71.4 million people were enrolled in Medicaid, according to preliminary CMS data. An additional 7.3 million were enrolled in CHIP. Together, the two programs covered nearly 41.4 million adults and 37.4 million children, or 23% of the US population.[28] Medicaid is a joint federal and state program and is the single largest source of health coverage in the United States.

For our purposes, in this chapter I will focus on Wisconsin's Medicaid program, benefits and eligibility. State Medicaid programs have distinct differences, and I will provide some contrasts and comparisons throughout this chapter.

A. New Policy, Benefits, and Eligibility Changes Enacted in 2025's One Big Beautiful Bill Act Medicaid Legislation

A major news item throughout the first half of 2025 focused on discussion of possible legislative cuts to coverage, eligibility, and benefits within the Medicaid program. The One Big Beautiful Bill Act (OBBBA) includes major reforms and drastic cuts to Medicaid and the Supplemental Nutrition Assistance Program (SNAP). The non-partisan Congressional Budget Office (CBO) has projected the following cuts to Medicaid and SNAP as a result of the OBBBA's passage into law.[29]

- According to the American Hospital Association, the proposed changes would reduce federal Medicaid support by over $700 billion across a ten-year period and could lead to coverage losses for millions of individuals
- Overall, 10.9 million individuals may be uninsured by 2034
- The Act will reduce federal spending on SNAP by $287 billion over ten years

1. Medicaid Work Requirements

Under the OBBBA able-bodied adults aged 19 to 64 will be required to either work, volunteer, study, or train for at least 80 hours per month to qualify for Medicaid. The bill includes exemptions for parents of children under 15, pregnant women, and those medically certified as physically or mentally unfit for employment. Medicaid enrollees will face more frequent eligibility reviews, possible care copay costs up to $35 per visit and be subject to more paperwork and verification checks, making it harder to apply for or maintain coverage. The 10.9 million people becoming uninsured projected by CBO will not be due to lack of employment but instead will become uninsured because of the bureaucratic hoops they would need to jump through to prove employment.[30] SNAP recipients are also facing similar work requirements, which could begin as soon as 2025. In 2028, for the first time, states with high error rates for providing SNAP benefits must pay up to 15% of SNAP costs.[31] These and other cuts offset the rising government costs associated with making permanent the tax cuts implemented during the first Trump administration. Other impacts from the OBBBA include states receiving less federal funding for

Medicaid beginning in 2028, which will cause states to likely eliminate some benefits, tighten enrollment, or add other cost-cutting changes.

The OBBBA work requirements are different than the work incentives discussed below in the Wisconsin Medicaid buy-in program for people with disabilities. Those are true incentives such as the provision of personal assistance in the workplace and not requirements being imposed on some Medicaid enrollees under the OBBBA. However, we will see how difficult these work rules have been for both enrollees and for states in implementing these requirements. The governors of both Iowa and Idaho in 2025 signed Medicaid work requirements into law similar to and in anticipation of the federal OBBBA.

During the first Trump administration, Arkansas attempted to implement work requirements for Medicaid recipients with consequences for noncompliance with reporting obligations. The attempt ended in 2019 when a federal court found the work requirement approval by CMS unlawful. Arkansas' work requirement attempt resulted in 18,000 people losing Medicaid coverage, primarily due to failure to regularly report the fact that they were working or document eligibility for an exemption. In 2025 Georgia is the only state with an active system using work requirements to establish Medicaid eligibility. Several states have continued to pursue work requirement waivers despite data showing that most Medicaid adults are working or face barriers to work. Among adults with Medicaid who are under age 65 and do not have Medicare or Supplemental Security Income (SSI), 91% are working, or are not working due to an illness, caregiving responsibilities, or school attendance.[32]

B. Medicaid Overview

In most states, if you have a disability and you receive Supplemental Security Income, also known as SSI, you are automatically eligible for Medicaid. Unlike Medicare, Medicaid serves every component of the US population from Neonatal-Intensive-Care-Unit-reliant (NICU) infants to impoverished elderly, unhoused adults, kids in foster care, low-income adults, and those with disabilities.

Medicaid eligibility has expanded in numerous ways throughout its history. Infants born to mothers eligible for Medicaid are automatically enrolled at birth and remain on Medicaid if their mother's income continues to fall within Medicaid eligibility limits, which vary by state. In 2021, Medicaid covered 41% of US births and nearly half of America's children receive care through the program.[33]

In Wisconsin 35% of all births in 2021 were covered by Medicaid, totaling 21,527 births. Louisiana had the most births financed by Medicaid at 61%. Utah finances the least at 21%.[34] Each state has their own eligibility criteria for Medicaid, considering factors such as income, family size, disability status, and age. While most states offer the full Medicaid package of benefits available to all beneficiaries, the specific benefits available to pregnant individuals vary from state to state. For example, Wisconsin is one of 11 states to cover both childbirth education classes and infant parenting classes for individuals enrolled in the state's Prenatal Care Coordination program.

One in five (20%) kids living in the United States – more than 14.5 million children total – has special health care needs, according to the National Survey of Children's Health as reported by the Ann Casey Foundation.[35] Children within this group are more likely to experience chronic physical, developmental, behavioral, or emotional conditions and require more care and services than children generally. Their needs result from a range of conditions, such as Down syndrome, cerebral palsy, and autism. They may require services such as nursing care to live safely at home, therapies to address developmental delays, and mental health counseling. Almost half of children with special health care needs rely on Medicaid/CHIP.[36] Medicaid provides a wide range of medical and long-term services and supports (LTSS), many of which are not covered at all or only available in limited amounts through private insurance. Medicaid also makes coverage affordable for many children and their families with special health care needs.

Since 1984 federal law has guaranteed enrollment for infants born to Medicaid beneficiary mothers, known as deemed newborn coverage. This coverage begins at birth and continues uninterrupted through the first year of life. Children in foster care are also eligible for Medicaid until they age-out at age 18.

Together with the Children's Health Insurance Program (CHIP), Medicaid covers almost half of all children with special health care needs. Medicaid/CHIP is the only source of coverage for nearly four in ten children with special health care needs in the nation, while another 8% have Medicaid/CHIP to supplement private insurance. Just over half of children with special health care needs have private insurance as their sole source of coverage.[37]

Other Medicaid coverage pathways for children with disabilities are offered at state option. Reflecting different state policy choices, the share of children with special health care needs covered by Medicaid/CHIP varies by state from 15% to 67%. Medicaid's benefit package for children – Early and Periodic Screening, Diagnostic and Treatment Services (EPSDT) – covers physical and behavioral health services and long-term services and supports enable children with chronic needs to live at home with their families. Medicaid supplements special education services. It also fills coverage gaps and makes coverage affordable for privately insured children with special health care needs to supplement and fill gaps in coverage for those with high-cost needs.

Nearly two-thirds of Medicaid/CHIP-only children with special health care needs live in a household with income at or below 138% of the federal poverty level (FPL, less than $36,777/year for a family of three in 2025) compared to 7% of children with private coverage only. Federal Medicaid program rules cover children with household incomes up to 138% of the FPL, but all states opt to expand financial eligibility to higher income levels: as of January 2025, the median financial eligibility level for Medicaid/CHIP children nationally is 255% FPL ($69,956/year for a family of three). Some children with special health care needs qualify for Medicaid based solely on their family's low income. Other children with special health care needs may qualify for Medicaid through various disability-related pathways, which may expand income limits to 300% SSI (about $34,900/year for an individual, equivalent to about 222% FPL) or only consider the child's own, and not their parents', income.

C. Medicaid Eligibility

Wisconsin's and Other States' Medicaid, CHIP, and BHP Income Eligibility Standards (For selected MAGI groups, based on state decisions as of July 1, 2025)

Children Medicaid Ages 0-1	301%
Children Medicaid Ages 1-5	186%
Children Medicaid Ages 6-18	151%

Children Separate CHIP	301% (age 1 up to 19)
Pregnant Women Medicaid	301%
Pregnant Women CHIP	N/A
Adults (Medicaid) Parent/Caretaker	95%
Adults (Medicaid) Expansion to Adults	N0 / 95%

As of May 2025, the total enrollment in Wisconsin Medicaid programs equaled 1,271,853 persons.[38] Federal law requires state Medicaid programs to cover certain groups of individuals. Required groups include low-income families, qualified pregnant women and children, and individuals receiving Supplemental Security Income (SSI). States have additional options for coverage and may choose to cover other groups, such as individuals receiving home- and community-based services and children in foster care who are not otherwise eligible.

The Patient Protection and Affordable Care Act of 2010 (ACA) created the opportunity for states to expand Medicaid to cover nearly all low-income Americans under age 65. Eligibility for children was extended to at least 133% of the federal poverty level (FPL) in every state (most states cover children to higher income levels), and states were given the option to extend eligibility to adults with income at or below 133% of the FPL. Most states have chosen to expand coverage to adults, and those that have not yet expanded may choose to do so at any time. If you think you might be eligible, see if your state has expanded Medicaid coverage to low-income adults.

The share of children with special health care needs covered by Medicaid/CHIP varies by state. State eligibility limits pathways for children who qualify for Medicaid/CHIP based solely on their low income range from 175% FPL to 405%

FPL. Additionally, most disability-related Medicaid eligibility pathways are optional and vary across states. States must provide Medicaid to children who receive federal SSI benefits, but only an estimated 21% of children with disabilities covered by Medicaid/CHIP receive SSI.[39] This means that the vast majority of Medicaid children with special health care needs are eligible either based on their family's low income or through an optional disability-related pathway. Thirty-two states provide Medicaid/CHIP to under half of children with special health care needs living in their state, and 19 states, including DC, provide Medicaid/CHIP to over half of children with special health care needs living in their state. Factors that are likely to contribute to states covering more children with special health care needs include the following:

- state's income eligibility limits
- percentage of children with special health care needs living in low-income households
- the state's disability-related eligibility pathway options

D. Gaining Medicaid Eligibility

There are numerous means by which an individual in Wisconsin and across the states gains eligibility for Medicaid coverage. These include but are not limited to:

1. Pregnant women with household income up to 300% of FPL
2. Children 19 and under with household income up to 300% of FPL
3. Adults with household income up to 100% of FPL
4. Affordable Care Act Medicaid Expansion to 138% of FPL
5. Individuals who are blind
6. Individuals with disabilities or a family member in the household with a disability
7. Individuals who are 65 years of age or older.

Wisconsinites access Medicaid through several different entry points, from being a newborn of a Medicaid-eligible mom, kids in foster care, to a low-income childless adult and children and adults with disabilities needing complex care. The next several pages provide an overview of some of those Medicaid coverage categories and eligibility criteria.

1. Low Birthweight Newborns' Eligibility

Social Security provides SSI disability benefits to certain infants of low birth weight, whether or not they were born prematurely. A child weighing less than 1,200 grams (about 2 pounds, 10 ounces) at birth or a child weighing between 1,200 and 2,000 grams (about 4 pounds, 6 ounces) at birth and considered small for their gestational age will generally qualify. Qualifying for this federal program also depends on a family's income and resources. To obtain these benefits, parents will need to go through an interview at their local Social Security Administration (SSA) office. The NICU social worker will help parents understand this process and provide information on what to bring to the interview. For more information, review the Child Disability Starter Kit at the SSA website.

2. Children with Down Syndrome's Eligibility

According to the Disability Benefits Center, children with Non-Mosaic Down syndrome applying for Social Security Disability benefits have a good chance of a successful application on their first attempt more often. For those with Mosaic Down syndrome there is a slight chance that the initial application will be denied. If this is the case, an appeal of SSA's decision can be made to receive Social Security Disability benefits.

Many children born with Down syndrome receive SSI, which provides monthly cash payments to children and adults with disabilities from lower-income households. SSI is for people of all ages, so your child could receive benefits as an infant and continue to qualify throughout adulthood. SSI is a means-tested program, so a family's income and resources may not exceed a certain threshold. This benchmark will vary depending on whether or not both parents are in the household and how many children there are in addition to your child with Down syndrome. For example, a single parent with two other children is capped at $3,791 per month (about $45,000 per year) in earned income, while a two-parent family with two children will have a higher monthly income limit at $4,158 a month, or $50,000 per year. The SSA's website contains a current list of income limits according to family demographic and size. If the family's income falls within approved income limits, and the application is approved, the child will receive monthly payments as well as access to Medicaid for their health care needs in nearly every state.

a. How to Qualify for SSI with Down Syndrome

To qualify for benefits, any applicant usually needs to meet a listing in the Blue Book, the SSA's catalog of intellectually and/ or physically disabling conditions and the criteria for meeting each one. Down syndrome appears in section 110.06–Non-Mosaic Down syndrome.

The majority of children with Down syndrome have the "non-mosaic" variety, (Trisomy 21 or Translocation), meaning that they have an extra 21st chromosome on each cell in their body. These children are considered disabled from birth due to the intellectual, physical, and neurological conditions that often accompany Down syndrome. If your child is diagnosed with Mosaic Down syndrome, he or she could still qualify, but your application will be a little more complicated. Parents will need additional medical medical evidence proving that a physical or intellectual complication caused by Down Syndrome keeps your child from participating in usual activities. Some listings a child might meet include:

- 102.00: Covers hearing loss or vision impairment
- 104:00: Any cardiovascular disorders
- 112.00: Intellectual and mood disorders

For those children with Down syndrome, parents or guardians complete an SSI application and include filing financial documents that confirm the household income and resources. The application also includes medical evidence of the child's Down syndrome diagnosis. The latter may include:

- A karyotype analysis report to identify blood or body fluids for abnormal chromosomes often used to detect genetic diseases in the developing fetus, or
- Documented medical confirmation of a chromosome 21 translocation or trisomy in addition to the physical aspects of Down syndrome, or
- A report confirming that the child's functional capacity is consistent with non-mosaic Down syndrome and that an analysis was performed in the past

If the household's income falls within approved limits, the child will usually be approved for SSI benefits if the child's non-mosaic Down syndrome diagnosis is conclusive. Should the application be denied on financial grounds, applicants may reapply after the child turns 18, as adults with disabilities are evaluated based on their own income or resources. Note: the vast majority of SSI applications are turned down for financial reasons, not medical. This means that the child has a great chance of qualifying once he or she is 18 and their parents' income no longer counts towards the household limit.

For more information on how to apply for SSI benefits

on behalf of the child with Down syndrome, visit the SSA's website, or schedule an appointment to apply at your closest office (there are over 1300 locations nationwide). To gain more information about SSA benefits, parents can do so by calling the SSA toll-free at 1-800-772-1213. Monthly disability payments will make it easier for parents and guardians to meet the daily needs of their son or daughter and cover medical expenses, thereby giving their child the most fulfilling life possible.

3. Health Home Coverage for Medically-Complex Children's Diseases

In 2022 the Centers for Medicare & Medicaid Services (CMS), implemented the option for states to offer a Medicaid health home benefit for children with medically complex conditions. A Medicaid Health Home is for people who:

- Have two or more chronic conditions
- Have one chronic condition and are at risk for a second
- Have one serious and persistent mental health condition

Health home providers, according to CMS, operate under a "whole-person" philosophy and integrate and coordinate all primary, acute, behavioral health, and long-term services and supports the whole person. This optional benefit helps state Medicaid programs offer covered services in the home, including person-centered care management, care coordination, and patient and family support. Children with medically complex conditions like cerebral palsy, cystic fibrosis, blood diseases, and mental health conditions often require intensive care coordination and highly specialized treatment.

CMS's goal is that the Health Home option ensures that children and families can get coordinated, high-quality care – particularly children with complex medical conditions.

4. Children and Youth with Special Health Care Needs Program (CYSHCN)

The CYSHCN Program is for those who have or are at increased risk for a chronic physical, developmental, behavioral, or emotional condition and who also require health and related services of a type or amount beyond that required by children generally.

The CYSHCN Program works to improve systems of care for anyone from birth through age 21 with a chronic physical, developmental, behavioral or emotional illness or condition. Some examples include ADHD, asthma, autism spectrum disorders, childhood cancers, cerebral palsy, deafness or blindness, diabetes, Down syndrome, heart disease, and mental health conditions.

Wisconsin has five Children's Resource Centers to support families with CYSHCN and the providers who serve them. The regional centers offer free, confidential help to find information, identify services, connect to community resources, and navigate health care and service systems information including:

- Early identification and screening
- Diagnosticians
- Therapy providers
- Health care benefits and waivers
- Paying for what is needed
- Respite and childcare options
- Educational support and special education
- Recreational opportunities
- Support groups for parents, siblings, or individuals with Autism Spectrum Disorder
- Transition to adult health care

Children and Youth with Special Health Care Needs[40]
The CYSHCN serves Wisconsin families. In Wisconsin, over 220,000 kids (about 17.5%) have special heath care needs. Of these:

- More than 1 in 10 miss 11 or more days of school due to illness or injury.
- More than 1 in 6 families have a family member leave a job, take a leave of absence, or reduce work hours because of their child's health.
- About 1 in 10 families that are currently insured have insurance that doesn't meet their needs.
- About 1 in 5 families spend $1,000 or more each year for out-of-pocket medical expenses.

Other disability-related resources available in Wisconsin that assist individuals and families navigating disability services include the following:

- Wisconsin First Step, a useful resource for families providing a 24-hour information and referral hotline with an online resource database.
- Disability Rights Wisconsin (DRW), an information resource for individuals with disabilities and their families. DRW helps people with disabilities understand and access mostly public but also some private benefits, including Social Security, Medicaid, Medicare, and other health insurance.

5. Foster Children

Health insurance and Medicaid coverage for children in and aging out of foster care could be a subject on its own. I cannot discuss this subject without sharing some startling national statistics compiled by the organization For Others,[41] including:

- More than seven million children nationally are impacted by the child welfare system, and over 368,000 are in foster care

- 90% of these children will experience severe trauma
- About 50% will reunite with their biological families
- 25% will attempt suicide
- Of the 20,000 young adults who age out each year, 81% of young men will become incarcerated
- 71% of young women will be pregnant before their twenty-first birthday, with half of their children destined to be placed in the foster care system themselves
- 40% will be homeless within 18 months of aging out of Medicaid
- 97% of these young adults aging out of Medicaid will immediately enter into chronic poverty

Starting the discussion with the aging-out crisis for these children in foster care and Medicaid may seem out of place. But with those results in mind, let's look at Medicaid coverage and how that works for children in Medicaid with the understanding that aging-out is traumatic and extremely difficult to navigate, even with more attention on the issue than ever before.

Now that we have this important understanding of the trauma and heartbreaking outcomes endured by children within America's child welfare system we can begin to unravel coverage issues. The child welfare system encompasses children who are in or at-risk of entering foster care, living with relative caregivers, or adopted out of care. Medicaid provides essential care for foster children, including access to physical, mental, and oral health care. In fiscal year 2023, 546,159 children experienced substantiated abuse or neglect,[42] 186,602 children entered foster care, and a total of 368,530 were in foster care at the end of the fiscal year.[43] An estimated 99% of children in foster care have Medicaid coverage, either by virtue of their eligibility for federal funding of foster care placement through Title IV-E of the Social Security Act or through other eligibility pathways.[44]

Medicaid plays an essential role in accessing all forms of standard care, including mental health and substance use disorder treatment and traditional outpatient therapy to intensive inpatient services in settings such as Medicaid-certified psychiatric residential treatment facilities. Children in foster care can also benefit from Medicaid-funded Treatment Foster Care, a specialized clinical intervention providing trauma-informed mental health services.

Approximately 27% of children who exit foster care join an adoptive family. This included 53,665 children and youth in fiscal year 2022. Of those children adopted, 57% were adopted by their foster parent(s) and 33% by a relative.[45] As noted above, the trauma endured by children in foster care is pervasive and insidious, occurring before and during foster care and does not disappear on adoption day. Adopted children can have significant health needs that even private insurance is often unable to address. Children adopted from foster care whose families are eligible for Adoption Assistance for special needs adoption are categorically eligible for Medicaid. This coverage performs a critical role in supporting stable, healthy, and thriving adoptive families.

6. Long-Term Services and Supports (LTSS)

There are a dozen or more ways to access coverage of long-term care services through Medicaid and other coverage mechanisms. Navigating those mechanisms and understanding when and how individuals are or may become eligible is confusing and frustrating. It is so confusing and difficult to navigate that many Americans do not understand the health coverage that is available to them through Medicaid. LTSS services encompass care for older adults and people with disabilities who need support because of age; physical, cognitive, developmental, or chronic health conditions; or other functional limitations that restrict their abilities to care for themselves. LTSS is long-term care in the Medicaid space. Wisconsin has numerous long-term care programs under the LTSS umbrella from children to the oldest adults in need. Community-based LTSS programs help older adults and people with disabilities live at home or in local settings. The results include better health and maximum independence. Community-based LTSS also provides help and encouragement to family members caring for older adults and people with disabilities. These supports can include training, counseling, support groups, and respite care. A wide range of services to help people live more independently by assisting with personal and health care needs and activities of daily living, including the following:

- Eating
- Taking baths
- Managing medication
- Grooming
- Walking
- Transferring up and down from a seated position

Even though children with special health care needs covered by Medicaid/CHIP-only have greater health care needs, they are more likely than those with private insurance alone to report that their benefits are always adequate to meet their needs. Medicaid/CHIP benefits allow them to see needed providers, and that they meet their behavioral health needs, reflecting Medicaid's robust benefit package.

Medicaid is the primary payer for home and community-based services (HCBS) and plays a significant role in providing children with special health care needs the LTSS they need to live at home with their families. While unmet need for HCBS for people with disabilities predates the COVID-19 pandemic, the COVID-19 pandemic heightened the need for additional HCBS. The American Rescue Plan Act provides a temporary increase in federal Medicaid matching funds for state spending on HCBS. Congress chose not to extend HCBS funding under the OBBBA and instead cut funding and eligibility.

a. Katie Beckett Program

One example of an LTSS program for children is the Katie Beckett program, also known as the Tax Equity and Fiscal Responsibility Act (TEFRA) Waiver, for children under age 19. Eligible children include those who have disabilities or complex medical needs. It's especially helpful for children who are not eligible for Medicaid because of their parents' higher income or assets. This is because eligibility for the waiver only takes into account the income and assets of the child. As of this writing, the Katie Beckett Waiver has been enacted in some form in 24 states, including Wisconsin.

The name comes from Katie Beckett of Cedar Rapids, Iowa, who had spent most of the first three years of her life living in an Iowa hospital. When she was just five months old, Katie contracted viral encephalitis, a brain infection, and went into a coma. After recovering, she had partial paralysis that left her unable to breathe without a ventilator much of the day. At the time, Medicaid would only pay for the expensive treatment if she stayed in the hospital. Katie's family advocated that the best treatments and services for her needs were available at home and in a community setting. In 1981, President Ronald Reagan heard about her situation and changed the rule so she could go home. As Reagan noted, it cost significantly less — about one-sixth as much — for Beckett to receive the care at home, instead of in a hospital. The federal government created a special category within Medicaid coverage under the Katie Beckett Waiver for kids just like Katie.

The Katie Beckett program helps children who have complex medical needs, long-term disabilities, or mental health needs. The program serves children who want to receive home and community-based services instead of living in a hospital or institution. The children then receive the same level of care they would in a facility but in the setting of their choice, typically at home, surrounded by their family rather than in a facility. Those children eligible for Katie Becket may qualify even if they are not eligible for other Medicaid programs because of their parents' or guardians' income or assets or if they are covered by private health insurance. At the time the program was developed, federal officials figured there were, at most, 100-200 children like Beckett around the country. Most of them were not expected to live very long. But since then, more than a half-million children have received life-extending medical care at home under the Beckett waiver. Katie and her mother Julie became known as national advocates for people with disabilities.

b. *Children's Long-Term Support Program*

Another LTSS example is the Children's Long-Term Support (CLTS) Program, which helps children with disabilities and their families through supports and services that help children grow and live their best lives. It is a home and community-based service waiver. It uses a Medicaid waiver to fund services for kids with disabilities. A waiver lets states use Medicaid to fund additional non-medical services and sup-

ports services not normally offered. The CLTS Program aims to keep kids at home instead of at an institution. In 2022 the federal government renewed the CLTS Program for five more years. The CLTS Program offers a range of services, including:
- Home and Community-Based Services were created to assist children with disabilities gain independence in both their home and community
- Support and Service Coordinators who assist families in finding the services they need and navigating the program
- Family Resources such as the Wisconsin Wayfinder that support families of children with delays, disabilities, special health care needs, and mental health conditions. The CLTS Program helps keep children with disabilities at home rather than residing in an institution. The waiver program was renewed for five more years in 2022 by CMS

c. Family Care

The Family Care program is a Wisconsin long-term care waiver initiative for adults designed to assist older adults and individuals with disabilities in accessing the services they need to live in a home setting. The Family Care program is for personal (non-medical) care such as attendant care for people with disabilities, assistance with eating, dressing, and bathing. The program provides comprehensive support designed to the needs of its members, ensuring they receive quality care and assistance with daily activities. Family Care offers long-term care under one benefit program. Long-term care is a service or support a person may need because:
- They have a disability
- They are older
- They have a lasting (chronic) illness

To enroll in Family Care, you must:
- Be at least 18 years old
- Be a frail elder or an adult with a disability
- Be eligible for Medicaid
- Be functionally eligible. The Long Term Care Functional Screen helps confirm eligibility
- Have a long-term care condition that will last more than 90 days

d. Family Care Partnership Program

This Wisconsin program mixes health and long-term support services in home and community settings. The Partnership program is more comprehensive, including full medical care and prescription drugs. The goals of the Partnership are to:
- Improve the quality of health care and services while keeping costs low
- Increase the ways people can live in the community and increase the ability of people to make their own choices about their health care
- Reduce the division in the current health care delivery system to improve efficiency

Who is Eligible for Assistance and Resources Related to the Partnership Program?

Aging and Disability Resource Centers (ADRC) can help individuals determine if they qualify for Partnership. Partnership serves members who qualify for both Medicaid and Medicare. ADRCs help with issues that affect older adults, people with disabilities, and their families. ADRCs make it easy to learn about resources near you. Those who seek assistance in the Partnership program must:
- Be at least 18 years old
- Be a frail elder or an adult with a disability

- Be eligible for Medicaid
- Be functionally eligible for Partnership. The Long Term Care Functional Screen helps confirm eligibility
- Have a long-term care condition that will last more than 90 days
- Live in a county that offers Partnership

7. Autism

According to the Centers for Disease Control and Prevention, in 2024 1 in 31 US children have been identified with an autism spectrum disorder.[46] Physicians have become more attuned to the symptoms and behaviors associated with autism and have become more adept at identifying autism. "Without a doubt, we've become exceptionally efficient in this surveillance work," Zachary Warren stated in a CDC report released on April 15, 2025. The number of children identified with ASD has risen dramatically; in 2021 the prevalence stood at 1 in 44 children. In 2000 the CDC indicated this was roughly 1 in 150.[47] Children with autism may qualify for Medicaid if they meet certain criteria. To qualify for Medicaid, a child must have a disability, but currently there is no specific diagnosis of autism that qualifies a child for Medicaid. However, children with autism may qualify if they meet the criteria for another disability, such as intellectual disability or cerebral palsy. Medicaid eligibility also depends on income and assets, so children with autism who come from low-income families are more likely to qualify. If you think your child may be eligible for Medicaid, you can contact your state's Medicaid office, county human services department, ADRC, or the SSA to learn more about the eligibility requirements.

BadgerCare Plus is a Wisconsin health care program that helps low-income children, pregnant people, and adults in Wisconsin with low incomes to access health coverage through Medicaid. The largest component of Wisconsin's Medicaid program, BadgerCare Plus, covers nearly 900,000 people, about half of them children. Most adults on Badger-Care Plus make less than the poverty level, or $15,650 in 2025 for an individual.[48] BadgerCare Plus also covers people during pregnancy and the postpartum period who have incomes less than three times the poverty level. The program covers things like routine medical exams, immunizations, prenatal care, and diagnostic physician visits. In addition, the program covers hospital care, prescription drugs, rehabilitation services, laboratory tests such as bloodwork, diagnostic services such as X-rays, and vision care, like contact lenses.

8. Medicaid Purchase Plan (MAPP)

MAPP is a Medicaid buy-in program for people in Wisconsin and offers Medicaid health care coverage to adults with disabilities who work or want to work. The Medicaid Purchase Plan in 2025 had enrollment of greater than 30,000 individuals. That enrollment number, however, includes thousands of individuals who are not seeking to maximize employment. However, the work incentives are there if enrollees choose to embrace them. With MAPP, people with disabilities can pursue employment and the following:

- Earn more income and have more assets than other Medicaid programs for people with disabilities
- Save earnings in Independence Accounts, helping enrollees reach personal and financial goals with an asset limit up to $15,000, rather than just $2,000 under standard Medicaid
- May save up to half of their gross annual earnings in an Independence Account that won't count for the $15,000 asset limit
- Are financially eligible for Medicaid Long-Term Care

(Family Care or IRIS [Include, Respect, I Self-Direct]) with no cost-share

To be eligible for MAPP, individuals must:
- Have a disability determination from the Disability Determination Bureau
- Live in Wisconsin
- Be at least 18 years old (no maximum age limit)
- Meet the work requirement
- Have less than $15,000 in countable assets excluding one home and one vehicle
- Have countable monthly income less than 250% of the Federal Poverty Level for the group size (applicant + spouse + dependent children). Only half of someone's earned income is counted plus unearned income. Additional deductions may apply

MAPP Work Requirements

MAPP is for people with disabilities who want to work and keep their Medicaid benefits. You can meet the work requirement if you receive wages from an employer, are self-employed, or have an informal work arrangement with someone you know. For individuals looking for employment, it is possible to meet the work requirement for up to 12 months by enrolling in the Health and Employment Counseling (HEC) Program. For self-employed individuals, it is not required that the business makes a profit, but it does have to create compensation at least once in a calendar month. Informal work arrangements must be regular and compensated at an equivalent of the minimum wage or greater. These work requirements allow individuals to maintain access to Medicaid at higher income levels or to explore work possibilities for individuals like Jay and Cassie discussed later in Part II of this book.

MAPP benefits and health coverage access are the same as those for other Medicaid members. For people enrolled in MAPP, they may also be eligible to receive long-term care services and supports through Family Care, Family Care Partnership, PACE (Program of All-Inclusive Care for the Elderly), IRIS, or the Children's Long-Term Support program.

9. Wisconsin Well Woman Program (WWWP)

The Wisconsin Well Woman Program (WWWP) is designed to assist women with little or no health insurance in obtaining screenings for breast and cervical cancers. The program offers free tests, including mammograms and Pap tests, for women aged 40 to 64 who qualify. Additionally, it provides Medicaid coverage for those diagnosed with breast or cervical cancer. The WWWP is part of the CDC's National Breast and Cervical Cancer Early Detection Program, ensuring comprehensive support for women's health. Eligibility is limited to women with incomes at or below 250% of the federal poverty level. In 2025 the enrollment in the Well Woman Program stands at about 270, indicating perhaps some Wisconsin women are missing out on helpful services.

E. Children's Health Insurance Program (CHIP)

In 1997 Congress enacted the Children's Health Insurance Program, known as CHIP, to provide comprehensive benefits to children. CHIP is a state-federal partnership with states administering CHIP within broad guidelines established by CMS. CHIP provides health insurance for uninsured children in low-income families that cannot afford private coverage and do not qualify for Medicaid.

In Wisconsin and most states, CHIP generally applies to children in households with an income above 150% of the FPL, although this threshold varies by the age of the child. CHIP is separate from Medicaid, providing states the flexibility to design their own program. As a result, benefits vary by state and by the type of CHIP program. However, all states must provide well-baby and well-child care, dental coverage, behavioral health care, and vaccines. In some states, CHIP covers pregnant women. States can either provide the same Medicaid benefit package as provided for children under each state's Medicaid state plan and/or section 1115 demonstration program. Section 1115 of the federal Medicaid statute provides the Department of Health and Human Services (DHHS) the authority to approve experimental, pilot, or demonstration projects that promote the objectives of the Medicaid and CHIP programs. Under this authority, DHHS may waive certain provisions of the Medicaid law to give states additional flexibility to design and improve their programs.

To be eligible for CHIP coverage, a child must be:
- Under 19 years of age
- Uninsured (determined ineligible for Medicaid, and not covered through a group health plan or creditable health insurance)
- A citizen or meet immigration requirements
- A resident of the state
- Eligible within the state's CHIP income range, based on family income

Between 2017 and 2021, 58% of youth with disabilities, ages 12-18, were publicly insured. For young adults with disabilities, ages 19-25, the percentage dropped to 43%.[49] This decline in public insurance coincides with the ending of CHIP eligibility at age 19 and the ending of childhood Medicaid eligibility between 19 and 21, depending on the state. For a sizeable population of young adults with disabilities (13%), especially Black young adults, this shift all too often results in loss of insurance. Black young adults with disabilities experience higher rates of uninsurance than White young adults with disabilities (15% vs 11%).[50] On average, each year more than 500,000 babies in the Medicaid program were not counted as enrolled for at least 90 days continuously. Most states show a gap between the number of infants counted as eligible and the number continuously enrolled. The percentage varies substantially by state, ranging from a low of 6% to a high of 41% in fiscal year 2018.[51]

1. Early and Periodic Screening, Diagnostic and Treatment (EPSDT) Services

States that have a CHIP program must provide the Medicaid benefit for children and adolescents known as the EPSDT benefit. EPSDT provides a comprehensive group of prevention, diagnostic, and treatment services for low-income infants, children, and adolescents under age 21, as specified in section 1905(r) of the Social Security Act. The EPSDT benefit is designed to ensure that children receive preventive care to detect health problems early and avoid serious health concerns. Prevention services covered by CHIP include age-appropriate vaccines. Eligibility varies by state, but the upper eligibility levels range from as low as 170% of the Federal poverty level (FPL) up to 400% of the FPL. See Appendix I for 2025 FPL guidelines.

2. Access to Care and Service Utilization Among Children with Special Health Care Needs

Even though children with special health care needs covered by Medicaid or CHIP have greater health care needs, they are more likely than those with private insurance alone to report that their benefits are always adequate. To meet their needs Medicaid allows them to see needed providers compared to those with private insurance alone. The Medicaid/CHIP-only group also is more likely to report that their insurance meets their behavioral health needs compared to those with private insurance alone. These findings likely reflect Medicaid's robust benefit package for children, which includes acute and preventive services as well as LTSS and Home and Community-based Services (HCBS), which are typically not covered by private insurance. Medicaid's EPSDT benefit includes regular medical, vision, hearing, and dental screenings as well as the services necessary to correct or rectify physical or mental health conditions. These services must be provided for children, regardless of whether a state chooses to cover them for adults. Medicaid/CHIP-only children with special health care needs are less likely to have a usual source of sick and preventive care.

Medicaid provides essential coverage to vulnerable Americans who are ineligible for other forms of health insurance. Medicaid is the payor of last resort. Medicaid only pays for health care services if individuals are ineligible for employer-based health insurance, Medicare, workers compensation, the Affordable Care Act (ObamaCare), or essentially any other means, including long-term care insurance. If an individual has both Medicare and Medicaid, Medicare is primary and Medicaid is secondary. Medicaid is always the payer of last resort when considering other forms of coverage.

F. Aging Out of Medicaid and CHIP Coverage

The transition into adulthood leaves low-income youth with disabilities at risk of losing health insurance coverage, income supports, and continuity of care. The National Alliance to Advance Adolescent Health studied the experiences of youth and young adults with disabilities as they age out of Medicaid, the CHIP, the Supplemental Security Income (SSI) program, and Title V Programs for Children and Youth with Special Health Care Needs (CYSHCN).

As of March 2023, at the end of the Medicaid continuous enrollment condition, nearly 42 million children were enrolled in Medicaid and CHIP.[52] States are required to provide Medicaid coverage for children until they turn 19, and this program, along with the CHIP, has been instrumental in lowering the uninsured rate for children. However, once children are 19 years old, in many cases they lose their age-based Medicaid or CHIP eligibility and are typically subject to the much more limited Medicaid eligibility criteria for adults. States are only required to provide Medicaid to non-disabled adults under age 65 if they are a pregnant woman or a parent of a dependent child. While eligibility levels for pregnant women are generally in the same range as for children, income eligibility levels for parents are often set much lower than for children. Young adults who lose Medicaid or CHIP coverage after turning 19 are in danger of becoming uninsured and losing access to their health providers and the medical treatments they may need.

The implications of aging out as one becomes an adult create difficulties with employment, housing, and access to food concerns as SNAP benefits may end as well. For those losing Medicaid health coverage as they turn age 19, they can apply and enroll in an Affordable Care Act (Marketplace) plan as early as 60 days before the Medicaid or CHIP coverage ends to avoid a gap in coverage. An application can be made for a Marketplace plan after the Medicaid or CHIP coverage ends – individuals have 90 days after submitting an application to enroll in a plan that will start at the beginning of the next month after enrollment is completed.

Supplemental Nutrition Assistance Program (SNAP)

Formerly known as Food Stamps, SNAP provides a monthly cash stipend – loaded onto an electronic benefits transfer (EBT) card – that can be used to buy groceries at participating stores and farmers markets.

When applying and qualifying for the first time, the state SNAP office will send an official approval letter explaining how long the benefits will last: generally anywhere from one month to three years. The letter may call this time period an "active" or "certification" period.

G. Medicaid and Long-Term Care Implications

Under Wisconsin rules there are specific asset limits for what a spouse not eligible for Medicaid can keep for themselves and remain in their home if their spouse needs nursing care or assisted living care paid for by Medicaid because of their eligibility. As of 2026 the Community Resource Allowance in Wisconsin allows the "community spouse" or "well spouse" to keep up to 50% of the couple's assets, up to a maximum of $162,660 of countable assets while their spouse qualifies for Medicaid. The community spouse's income is not counted toward the nursing home applicant's eligibility. This number is a maximum. The "community spouse" can keep one home and a car.

For the spouse residing in the nursing home, their available assets are limited to $2,000 except for a small personal needs allowance. So, the spouse who wants to participate in Medicaid long-term care services must either transfer his or her income to the community spouse or use it to pay for nursing home or home care to get down to the $2,000 asset limit.

1. Estate Recovery

Estate recovery is the process for states to get paid back for long-term care Medicaid benefits. I'll provide the basics here and touch on some aspects that are important to consider. The Estate Recovery Program is mandatory under federal law and in Wisconsin allows the Wisconsin Department of Health Services to step in after an individual passes away and take money from their estate. That money would otherwise go to the deceased's family. State Medicaid long-term care programs expend millions each year covering elderly or disabled residents who need long-term care and cannot afford it.

There are exceptions, and consulting an estate law attorney well in advance of needing long-term care services is important. Long-term care insurance can be an especially useful means to protect assets from Medicaid estate recovery. By covering some or all of the costs of long-term care, these policies can help individuals avoid spending all their savings by paying out-of-pocket for long-term care. Estate recovery applies only to the Medicaid programs that provide long-term care. Anyone who is not elderly, blind, or disabled and is not receiving long-term care services shouldn't worry. That means estate recovery mostly affects Medicaid recipients (of any age) who live in nursing homes, and elderly Medicaid recipients who live at home or in assisted living and receive long-term care. If an individual uses private pay or long-term care insurance coverage to pay for long-term care instead of Medicaid, estate recovery does not apply. Advance planning and consulting an estate planning attorney are essential.

Estate recovery doesn't happen until the Medicaid recipient dies. If the recipient is survived by a spouse or a young or disabled child, estate recovery doesn't happen until *they* die. So spouses shouldn't worry they will be left destitute, and a young or disabled child's support won't be taken away. These are the most immediate concerns.

H. Waiver Programs Expand Medicaid Eligibility and Benefits

A Medicaid waiver is a provision in Medicaid law that allows the federal government to waive rules that allow states to expand Medicaid eligibility or services that typically apply to the Medicaid program. Waivers allow individual states, with federal approval, to accomplish certain goals, such as reducing costs, expanding coverage, or improving care for certain target groups, such as the elderly or special needs children.

Through waiver provisions states can provide services to their residents that wouldn't usually be covered by Medicaid. For instance, in-home care for people who otherwise must go to a residential care facility.

There are several different types of Medicaid waivers which serve various purposes. All waivers, no matter what type or state, are under the authority of Sections 1115 and 1915 of the Social Security Act.

Section 1115 Waivers: Often referred to as research and demonstration waivers, these allow states to temporarily test new innovations in care, services, and/or financing. For these waivers to be approved, they must be budget neutral for the federal government – meaning that the federal government will not spend more because of the waiver than they would otherwise.

Section 1915(b) Waivers: "Freedom of choice waivers" allow states to provide care via managed care delivery systems. These organizations contract with state Medicaid agencies and are paid from the state Medicaid fund for providing health care services to the beneficiaries, thus limiting the individual's ability to choose their own providers.

Section 1915(c) Waivers: Home and Community-Based Services (HCBS) waivers are designed to allow states to provide home and community-based services to people in need of long-term care. This means they can stay in their own home or in a community setting (such as a relative's home or a supported living community) instead of going into a nursing facility.

Each state can develop its own waiver programs, so rules and eligibility criteria vary state-to-state. As examples, Medicaid waivers help pay for standard medical and non-medical care, including personal care services, respite care, and adult daycare.

1. Include, Respect, I Self-Direct (IRIS)

IRIS is a 1915(c)-waiver program for adults with disabilities and elderly people in Wisconsin. It is a self-directed program. Individuals enrolled in IRIS have the freedom to decide how they want to live their life, the services they receive and when, where, and how they receive them. The IRIS program is a Medicaid long-term care program for older adults and adults with disabilities in Wisconsin. It is a self-directed program, which means participants have the freedom to decide how they want to live their lives. Wisconsin's Department of Health Services can offer the IRIS program thanks to the 1915(c) HCBS waiver from the federal Centers for Medicare

& Medicaid Services (CMS). The IRIS waiver program was recently renewed and is in effect through 2030.

More Medicaid Thoughts

And before I conclude the Medicaid discussion, I think you can agree Medicaid covers a wide array of Americans, providing essential health coverage and benefits. Because of this, I believe very strongly that Medicaid-for-All is a more compelling health care expansion option than the Medicare-for-All proposals promoted by Presidential candidates in the recent past. Because Medicaid providers receive lower reimbursement rates than for Medicare, commercial, or ACA coverage, financing and provider reimbursement alterations would be needed. Most states administer their Medicaid benefits through a managed care contracting process with health insurers. This competitive Medicaid contracting process could serve as the basis for Medicaid-for-All, as the basic system already exists. That may be a sneak peek for a follow-up effort I may undertake in another book.

Chapter V

Medicare

First and foremost, it is important to understand that Medicare only covers long-term care needs under VERY limited circumstances. Medicare covers skilled nursing facility care for a limited period, typically up to 100 days per benefit period. Medicare does NOT cover custodial nursing home care for long-term stays. Instead, Medicare only covers skilled nursing care which is not the same as care provided for long-term nursing home stays. Medicare will only cover care received in a skilled nursing facility if an individual has a qualifying inpatient hospital stay. This means a prior medically necessary inpatient hospital stay of at least three days in a row immediately prior to the skilled nursing facility stay.

> **Medicare, Navigation Stress, and Misunderstandings**
> "More than half of older adults (56%) say it is difficult and stressful to navigate the current health care system, while nearly two in three (62%) say health insurance plans provide too many confusing choices. Research has shown that more than half (55%) mistakenly believe Medicare will cover a long-term stay in a nursing home."[53]

Medicare Coverage Options

Components	Description	Eligibility
Medicare Part A (hospital insurance)	Part A helps pay for inpatient care at: • Hospitals • Skilled nursing facilities • Hospice Part A also covers some outpatient home health care.	Part A is free for individuals who worked and paid Medicare taxes for at least ten years. You may also be eligible because of your current or former spouse's work.
Medicare Part B (medical coverage)	Part B helps cover: • Services from doctors and other health care providers • Outpatient care • Home health care • Durable medical equipment • Some preventive services	Most people pay a monthly premium for Part B. The exact premium depends on the individual's income level.
Medicare Advantage (Part C)	Part C is known as Medicare Advantage. It's an alternative to Parts A and B that bundles several coverage types, including Parts A, B, and usually D. It may also include: • Vision • Hearing • Dental insurance *Medicare Advantage plans replace Medicare entirely and cannot be supplemented by a Medicare supplement plan.	Individuals must sign up for Part A or Part B before enrolling in a Medicare Advantage plan. (Private companies run Parts C and D. The federal government approves each plan. Costs and coverage types vary by provider.)

Components	Description	Eligibility
Medicare Part D (Prescription drug coverage)	Medicare Part D (Prescription drug coverage) Part D provides an outpatient prescription drug optional benefit to older adults and people with long-term disabilities in Medicare who enroll in private plans, including stand-alone prescription drug plans (PDPs). These plans supplement traditional Medicare and Medicare Advantage prescription drug plans (MA-PDs) that include drug coverage and other Medicare-covered benefits.	Individuals must sign up for Part A or Part B before enrolling in a private Part D plan.
Medicare Supplement Plans (Medigap)	Medicare Supplement Plans (Medigap) are private insurance policies that that provide supplemental coverage of some otherwise non-covered items. Each plan has a letter assigned to it and offers the same basic benefits. You must pay a premium for Medigap insurance in addition to your Medicare Part B premium and Medicare Part D.	Individuals purchase a supplement plan to help pay for the out-of-pocket costs of original Medicare. These plans are offered by companies that contract with Medicare. These plans may include Part D as well.

An important way that Medicare is different than Medicaid is how one becomes eligible and its differing components or Parts that align with certain types of coverage.

One of the greatest concerns, cited by 68% of older Americans, is not being able to afford future health and long-term care needs. Today, the average yearly cost for a private room in a nursing home is over $116,000.[54]

Medicare is government-provided health insurance available to people ages 65 and older and people under age 65 with certain disabilities. Unlike Medicaid, Medicare is solely regulated by the federal government and is a primary source of insurance for those over age 65. Medicare has its own unique terms that apply only to its plans and coverage. Knowing the nuances of Medicare and its own unique terms is important to maximizing its coverage and accessing the best plan for an individual's specific needs.

The year 2025 was the peak year the baby boom generation turns 65. Each day in 2025 11,400 Americans become age 65 and gain eligibility for Medicare. According to the US Census Bureau, by the year 2034 more Americans will be over age 65 than those younger than age 18.[55] This will apply further strains on the long-term care system and workforce.

Home health is covered under both Medicare Part A and B, depending on the covered person's circumstances. Home health encompasses a wide range of health care services that you can get in your home for an illness or injury. Home health care is usually less expensive, more convenient, and just as effective as care received in a hospital or skilled nursing facility (SNF). As noted in the table above Medicare Part A provides Hospital Insurance coverage while and/or Medicare Part B provides coverage for physician services and eligible home health services, as long as a person needs part-time or intermittent skilled services and you're "homebound," which means:

- You have trouble leaving home without mobility assistance like a cane or wheelchair because of an illness or injury
- Leaving your home isn't recommended because of your condition
- You have trouble leaving your home because it's a major effort

Covered home health services include medically necessary, part-time or intermittent skilled nursing care, like:

- Wound care for pressure sores or a surgical wound
- Intravenous or nutrition therapy
- Injections
- Monitoring serious illness and/or an unstable health status
- Physical therapy
- Occupational therapy
- Speech-language pathology services
- Medical social services

Traditional Medicare

Traditional Medicare, also known as Original Medicare, is a federal health insurance program primarily for retired people over age 65 that includes two main parts:

- Part A (Hospital Insurance): Covers inpatient hospital stays, SNF care, for up to 21 days after a three-day inpatient hospital stay, hospice care, and some home health care.
- Part B (Medical Insurance): Covers outpatient care, doctor visits, preventive services, and some medical supplies. Traditional Medicare operates on a fee-for-service basis,

meaning the government pays directly for health care costs incurred by beneficiaries. It became available in 1966 and is designed to provide essential medical services to eligible individuals.

For most individuals, Medicare Part A has no monthly premium if the following requirements have been met. An individual must work ten years (40 quarters) paying Medicare taxes to receive zero-premium Medicare Part A. If you do not meet this requirement, individuals could pay up to $518 for Medicare Part A each month in 2025, a slight increase from the $505 enrollees faced throughout 2024.

Medicare enrollment periods sign up for the various parts of Medicare. Below, we'll discuss some of the most important Medicare Enrollment Periods.

Initial Enrollment Period: Lasts for seven months. It begins three months before you turn 65 and lasts up to three months after your date of birth.

Special Enrollment Period: Occurs due to qualifying life events. The most common reason is if you are over 65 and terminate private insurance through your or your spouse's employer if the employer has 20 or more employees. In this case (and others), you are eligible for a Special Enrollment Period for Medicare.

General Enrollment Period: If you fail to apply for Medicare during your Initial Enrollment Period or Special Enrollment Period, this will allow you to still sign up for Medicare. This enrollment period begins on January 1 and runs through March 31 each year.

Automatic Enrollment: You may automatically enroll in Part

A and Part B at 65 if you begin to receive retirement benefits from either the Railroad Retirement Board or Social Security.

In addition to their premiums, Medicare Part A has a deductible and copayments, while Medicare Part B has a deductible. If an individual purchases a Medigap or Medicare supplement plan, the Medicare Part A costs and Part B deductible may be covered up to 100%.

It is important to also understand that Medicare Part B only covers 80% of an individual's medical costs. If you do not have a Medicare Supplement plan, you must pay the remaining 20% out-of-pocket. Traditional Medicare includes deductibles, and coverage is generally at 80%.

Medigap/Medicare Supplement Plans

Medicare Supplement (Medigap) Plans are secondary coverage that pays after traditional Medicare pays. They will cover the 20% a patient is responsible for with outpatient services. These supplemental plans will also cover additional out-of-pocket costs such as deductibles and copays.

Supplemental coverage can make a big difference in filling the gaps in coverage not provided through traditional Medicare, especially if an individual incurs an illness or injury resulting in numerous hospital and physician charges.

Medicare Advantage (MA)

Private insurance companies offer Medicare Advantage plans that Medicare approves. Medicare Advantage plans offered through Medicare Part C combine Part A hospital coverage and Part B doctor and outpatient services. Some Medicare Advantage plans also include Part D prescription coverage into one comprehensive plan.

In 2024 nearly 33 million Medicare beneficiaries were

enrolled in a Medicare Advantage plan, more than half, or 54%, of the eligible Medicare population, according to the Kaiser Family Foundation.[56] If an individual decides to get coverage through a Medicare Advantage plan, they will still have to enroll in Medicare parts A and B. Then they can choose a Medicare Advantage plan and sign up with a private insurer. People may have several options, depending on your location. The average Medicare beneficiary had 42 Medicare Advantage plans to choose from for the 2025 plan year, according to the Kaiser Family Foundation.[57]

Medicare Advantage plans cover everything that Medicare parts A and B cover, but they may have different deductibles and copayments. Some Medicare Advantage plans provide additional coverage to people with chronic conditions. Provisions include meal delivery, shower grips, and wheelchair ramps for your home, plus transportation to and from doctors' offices.

Here are several important ways the Medicare Advantage program differs from traditional Medicare.

Payments differ between the two programs. In Medicare Advantage, insurers are paid a set amount per beneficiary, depending on their age and health status. Insurers then pay providers for beneficiaries' health expenses. Traditional Medicare uses the fee-for-service model, where providers are paid per service delivered with little incentive for efficiency or value.

Medicare Advantage plans typically offer enrollees a set network of providers for non-emergency care. Traditional Medicare enrollees can receive care from any provider that accepts Medicare. Most Medicare Advantage plans offer supplemental benefits not included in traditional Medicare. In 2022 almost all Medicare Advantage plans offered vision, hearing, fitness, and dental benefits, and some provided discount cards for over-the-counter health items not covered by insurance.

Medicare enrollees can choose to add Medicare supplement plans to cover additional costs not covered by Medicare Parts A and B.

The main reasons MA and traditional Medicare enrollees choose their coverage differ. The top reason MA enrollees say they chose their coverage was for more benefits, followed by out-of-pocket cost limits. The top reason traditional Medicare enrollees said they chose their coverage was more provider choice, according to a survey from the Commonwealth Fund.[58] Special needs Medicare Advantage plans, described below, offer care for members dually eligible for Medicare and Medicaid and members with certain chronic conditions. How does an individual decide whether to enroll in a Medicare Advantage plan versus traditional Medicare? Are enrollees more satisfied with one over the other?

Traditional Medicare and MA enrollees generally report equal satisfaction with their coverage but have different worries about their health care, a survey from eHealth found. Medicare supplement enrollees were more likely to list having their Medicare benefits reduced as their top future health care worry. Medicare Advantage enrollees were more likely to report concerns about not being able to afford their care.[59] Aging and Disability Resource Centers (ADRC's) are perhaps the best source of information on available plans and benefits. Perhaps the most important consideration in making a decision is which health plans offer a provider you trust is to provide your care.

Dual Eligible Special Needs Plan (D-SNP)

Many individuals eligible for Medicare have lower incomes and are also dually eligible for Medicaid and can gain health coverage through D-SNP health plans. A D-SNP is an optional program within Medicare Advantage plans for individuals who are eligible for both Medicare and Medicaid coverage. This plan coordinates care among Medicare and Medicaid to improve care more effectively while also lowering costs. Medicare SNPs cover the same Medicare services that all Medicare Advantage plans must cover. States may vary in determining their eligibility category, therefore, there may be state-specific differences in the eligibility levels in comparison to those listed below. Each state's Medicaid program runs three cost-reduction programs which allow slightly higher incomes and asset levels than straight Medicaid eligibility. These programs are Qualified Medicare Beneficiary (QMB), Specified Low-Income Medicare Beneficiary (SLMB), and Qualifying Individual (QI). These Medicaid financial eligibility categories allow for dual eligibility of both Medicaid and Medicare for those over age 65 and at lower income levels. It is best to contact the local ADRC to determine eligibility for these programs, but the basics are as follows:

- QMB – If a person is eligible for Medicare and meets the income and asset eligibility requirements for the QMB program, their state's QMB program will pay all of your Medicare Part A and Part B premiums, deductibles, and coinsurance.
- SLMB – If a person's income is just a bit too high to qualify for QMB benefits, they may still be eligible for the SLMB program. The resource limits for SLMB eligibility are the same as for a QMB, but the income limits are 20% higher.
- Qualifying Individual (QI) – If an individual's income is too high to qualify for SLMB benefits, they may still be eligible for financial help under the QI program. The resource limits for eligibility are the same as a QMB or SLMB, but the income limits are 80% higher, depending on the program.

Medicare D-SNPs may also cover extra services tailored to the special groups they serve, like extra days in the hospital with benefits varying depending on the plan. In addition, it should be noted that many individuals, about 25% of those on D-SNP plans, also benefit from SNAP for food assistance because of their low incomes.

Program of All-Inclusive Care for the Elderly (PACE)

PACE is a national program that provides older adults with health care, long-term care, prescription drugs, and other services. PACE aims to help its members live in a home setting for as long as they can. In Wisconsin PACE is only an option for people who live in Kenosha, Milwaukee, Racine, and Waukesha counties.

PACE Programs help seniors who would otherwise be required to live in a Medicaid nursing home to continue living at home in or in assisted living residences. PACE is available in 33 states including Wisconsin and is a comprehensive Medicare and Medicaid (dual eligible) program. In some areas of the country, notably the mid-Atlantic states, PACE Programs are called LIFE Programs (Living Independence for the Elderly). These programs are particularly relevant to persons applying for Medicaid, as the vast majority of PACE recipients (approximately 90%) are "dual eligible" (eligible for both Medicare and Medicaid).

Medicare Benefits for People with Disabilities

Navigating potential health care plans and understanding Medicare eligibility can be challenging, especially for individuals under age 65 who have a disability. Individuals under the age of 65 with a disabling condition, approved through the disability determination process, may qualify for Medicare coverage. A qualifying disability is almost any health condition that prevents a person from being able to work enough to access employer-sponsored health care benefits. Before enrolling in Medicare, individuals must first receive Social Security Disability Insurance for two years. However, if diagnosed with either end-stage renal disease or amyotrophic lateral sclerosis, also known as ALS or Lou Gehrig's disease, the 24-month waiting period is waived.

Medicare was originally established to provide coverage for older adults who lost employer-based insurance when they retired at age 65. Starting in the 1970s, it also covers those under 65 who receive Social Security disability benefits. Medicare is funded through federal Social Security taxes and does not require income limits to qualify for coverage. Conversely, Medicaid is a needs-based program that serves low-income individuals. It's funded through a mix of federal, state and local taxes. There are no age restrictions to qualify for Medicaid, and the program is administered at the state level.

Both Social Security Disability Insurance (SSDI) and Supplemental Security Income (SSI) are administered by the Social Security Administration (SSA) and provide assistance to people who meet the federal agency's requirements for disabilities.

SSDI:

Individuals with disabilities and family members – including a spouse, divorced spouse, children under the age of 16, and adult children who were disabled before age 22 – can receive benefits if you are insured. Your eligibility is based on how long and how recently you worked and whether you paid Social Security taxes on those earnings. Everyone eligible for Social Security Disability Insurance (SSDI) benefits is also eligible for Medicare after a 24-month qualifying period. The first 24 months of disability benefit entitlement is the waiting period for Medicare coverage. During this qualifying period for Medicare, the beneficiary may be eligible for health insurance through a former employer. The employer should be contacted for information about health insurance coverage. For economic reasons, the 24-month waiting period is waived for people with amyotrophic lateral sclerosis (ALS) or end-stage renal disease because these diseases progress rapidly. SGA refers to the level of work activity that can affect eligibility for SSDI. SGA serves as a threshold to evaluate whether a person with a disability can engage in substantial work despite their condition. In 2026 the SGA limit is $1,690 per month ($2,830 if the individual is blind). If an individual earns above this amount, they are generally considered to be engaging in SGA, which may disqualify them from receiving disability benefits.

SSI:
Adults and children who meet the SSA's requirements for a qualifying disability and have limited income and resources can receive benefits from the SSI program. The two programs are different but have the same medical requirements. However, if an individual meets the nonmedical requirements established by the SSA, then they may be eligible for monthly benefits if the medical condition is expected to last at least a year or is terminal. An application for benefits can be made at the SSA website.

Chapter VI

Veteran's Care

Individuals who served in the military are eligible for Veteran's Affairs health care. Coverage includes regular checkups with a primary care provider and appointments with specialists (like cardiologists, gynecologists, and mental health providers). Veterans can access services like home health and geriatric (elder) care with coverage for durable medical equipment such as wheelchairs and walkers, prosthetics, and prescriptions. Veterans can apply at va.gov and manage the health care benefits they earned. The available durable equipment my dad benefitted from was a wheelchair and a walker. He also received care at the VA, including routine annual vision screenings. Veteran's care issues are discussed specifically in the Part II journeys involving my dad and Jay.

As of 2023, there were around 15.8 million military veterans in the United States. That means that around 6% of adults in the US were veterans at that time.[60] This figure rises considerably with age, with military veterans accounting for around a quarter of men aged 65 to 74 years and around 42% of men aged 75 years and older. Veterans have often been exposed to unique stressors and dangers that put them at higher risk for various physical and mental health issues. For this reason, veteran health and veteran access to health care services is an especially important topic. In 2022 it was estimated that around 35% of civilian veterans aged 21 to 64 years in the United States had a service-connected disability.

There is an Aid and Attendance Benefit that provides benefits for war-era veterans and their surviving spouses who require the regular attendance of another person to assist in at least two of the daily activities of living such as eating, bathing, dressing and undressing, transferring, and toileting. Those who are eligible receive up to $3,740 monthly.

All veterans who meet basic service and discharge requirements and who were exposed to toxins and other hazards while serving our country – at home or abroad – are now eligible for VA health care. Veterans who served in the Vietnam War, Gulf War, Iraq, Afghanistan, or any other combat zone after 9/11 are included. Veterans can use services through the Department of Veteran's Affairs to apply for and manage the VA benefits and services like health care, disability, education, and more. Veteran's Affairs offers confidential support for veterans, service members, and their families at no cost. Services include readjustment counseling, which is offered to make a successful transition from military to civilian life or counseling after a traumatic event experienced in the military. Individual, group, marriage, and family counseling is offered in addition to referrals and connections to other VA or community benefits and services. Vet Center counselors and outreach staff, many of whom are Veterans themselves, are experienced and prepared to discuss the tragedies of war, loss, grief, and transition after trauma.

Veterans care eligibility includes those who:
- served in the active military, naval, or air service and didn't receive a dishonorable discharge
- enlisted after September 7, 1980, or entered active duty after October 16, 1981

- served 24 continuous months or the full period for which the individual was called to active duty, unless any of the descriptions below are true for the individual

This minimum duty requirement may not apply if any of these are true if an individual:

- is discharged for a disability that was caused – or made worse – by the active-duty service
- is discharged for a hardship or "early out"
- served prior to September 7, 1980
- is a current or former member of the Reserves or National Guard

Eligible individuals must have been called to active duty by a federal order and completed the full period for which they were called or ordered to active duty. If the individual had or has active-duty status for training purposes only, they do not qualify for VA health care.

If an individual served in certain locations and time periods during the Vietnam War era, they are eligible for VA health care. If they meet the basic service and discharge requirements and were exposed to toxins or other hazards while serving in the military – at home or abroad – they are eligible for VA health care. This includes all Veterans who served in the Vietnam War, Gulf War, Iraq, Afghanistan, or any other combat zone after 9/11.

Veterans who are ill or disabled are eligible for long-term care services including:

- 24/7 nursing and medical care
- Physical therapy
- Help with daily tasks (like bathing, dressing, making meals, and taking medicine)

- Comfort care and help with managing pain
- Support for caregivers who may need skilled help or respite care so they can work, travel, or run errands

This care is available in many different settings, some run by the VA and others run by state or community organizations. Veterans can receive care in the following settings:
- Nursing homes
- Assisted-living centers
- Private homes where a caregiver supports a small group of individuals
- Adult day health centers
- Veterans' own homes

VA services are more likely used by a veteran who is younger, female, unmarried, less educated, within a minority group, and more likely to have a lower household income than those who do not use the services for which they are eligible. Those receiving VA services are also more likely to have served longer in the military and in combat. VA users are more likely to screen positive for lifetime psychopathology, endorse current suicidality, and report enduring more traumas. VA users are also more likely to report more medical conditions, identify as having a disability, and score lower on measures of physical and cognitive functioning. The primary factor differentiating VA users from those that did not use VA was the presence of lifetime psychopathology.

Part I: Summary

The overview I have provided of the means to access and finance long-term care services is my best attempt at describing the challenging and incongruent long-term care system. This overview provides a basis for discussion of four distinct personal journeys in long-term care and the challenges each of these four families continue to face in managing their loved one's care.

The first of four long-term care journeys involves my parents, an elderly middle-class couple who have long-term care insurance. Each of the four journeys in Part II are examples of how individuals and their families struggled through the complexity of LTC resources and programs depicted in Part I.

PART II

Long-Term Care Journeys

Journey 1

Don and Kate – Elderly Couple Residing in a Long-Term Care Facility

After my father, Don, retired in 1995, he and my mother, Kate, had the foresight to purchase long-term care insurance to preserve their assets. They had seen both their parents in nursing home care at the end of their lives and saw their assets depleted by paying for care without the protection of long-term care insurance. My parents had worked hard to advance into the middle class from their humbler beginnings and wanted to preserve their investments to pass on to their three children, seven grandchildren, and eight great-grandchildren.

My mother was a devoted caretaker of her family throughout our lives. She worked part-time from about age 39 to her retirement at age 62 as a bank teller, secretary, financial specialist, and technical writer. In 2018 Mom was diagnosed with mild dementia. Her mother died at the age of 86 and had memory issues and dementia for the last seven or so years of her life. That fact bothered Mom incessantly, causing her difficulty over the decades as she worried about possible dementia when she would forget things. Dementia and Alzheimer's disease are insidious illnesses, robbing individuals of their confidence as they age.

After Mom's dementia diagnosis, I reached out to the Alzheimer's Association of Wisconsin for resources to help Dad read about the illness and what to expect as Mom's condition progressed. I am proud that I have served on the organization's board of directors since 2023. In 2024 approximately 120,000 individuals in Wisconsin were living with either dementia or Alzheimer's disease.[61] In addition, Mom was diagnosed with anxiety and has had obsessive/compulsive tendencies. She started dealing with hearing loss in her 70s, requiring the use of hearing aids at age 79. Remembering to charge her hearing aid batteries and putting her hearing aids in was a challenge due to her forgetfulness.

Dad is an Air Force veteran and retired after 35 years as a US Postal Service mail carrier. In his job as a mail carrier, he drove 100 miles a day, delivering mail to more than 400 homes. He drove in a difficult driving position from the car's passenger seat with his left leg stretched across the vehicle operating both the gas and brake pedals. In his early 80s Dad was diagnosed with spinal stenosis, perhaps stemming from the uncomfortable driving position he was in for several hours each workday. But the spinal stenosis may have also stemmed from his scoliosis. Dad also tells the story of his exit physical when his four-year Air Force commitment ended. The physician conducting the physical asked Dad how he was accepted into military service with the severity of his spine curvature. Dad said it was never mentioned or revealed that he had scoliosis until that moment. Because of his military service he can access services at Veterans Affairs medical facilities. As an example, as he aged into his mid-80s, he slowed down considerably, needing a cane as he began having difficulty walking longer distances. He was able to get a walker and then later a wheelchair from his local VA clinic as he needed more than just his cane as his mobility declined.

When Mom was in her 70s, she would often think back to her own mother's forgetfulness and advancing dementia as she reached and progressed into her 80s. As Mom approached her 80s, she would often lament that she thought it was also happening to her. When Mom was 81, her physician suggested having a cognitive assessment. When she was then diagnosed with dementia, this exacerbated her worry and anxiety. Our family became increasingly concerned about her forgetfulness, as she increasingly forgot where she put things and how to do routine tasks.

As Mom aged, she became more forgetful and aware of this increasing difficulty over time. As her hearing worsened, Mom became fixated on cochlear implants as an option to improve her hearing. Despite going to a specialist three times and learning that the implants were not a viable option for her, after a while she would forget that news and want to pursue them again. We could not convince her otherwise, until her dementia progressed further, and she forgot about it entirely. The combination of anxiety, worsening hearing loss, and dementia proved to be extremely frustrating for Mom, causing instances of anxiety, inducing dizzy spells, some falls, and emergency room visits. Luckily, the fall instances in her early eighties did not result in any broken bones, despite her history of osteoporosis.

At one point Mom made a pan of brownies in preparation for her children's visit for the Christmas holidays. After her children arrived, Mom, Dad, and my sisters searched everywhere for the brownies as she forgot where she had put them when she wanted to serve them. During the entire holiday no one was able to find them. Time passed and Mom mentioned several months later to my sister Sue that they had finally found the brownies in a cupboard no one had searched. She said she and Dad had eaten them. The fact that they ate five-six-month-old brownies was obviously very disconcerting to us. We decided that Mom's cooking was becoming a concern and a possible danger. My sisters and I also began asking more about what food they were eating, and Dad said he had been going to McDonalds for hamburgers or the local convenience store routinely.

My sisters and I began cooking for them and storing the food in their freezer in the basement. Mom would forget that this extra pre-prepared food was available in the basement, and Dad's mobility issues had worsened where he had difficulty with the stairs. There were literally two dozen frozen meals that were unused for months. In June 2020 we met with our parents and discussed their long-term care insurance policy. I then began researching how to use long-term care insurance based on my previous experience working in long-term care policy as a Medicaid policy analyst for the state of Wisconsin. I found key terms within the policy and researched their meaning including:

- Daily benefit amount
- Hands-on assistance
- Activities of daily living
- Elimination period
- Lifetime benefit

Long-term care insurance policies provide coverage of long-term care and nursing services in multiple settings for those who meet eligibility requirements related to dementia or need for hands-on assistance with two or more activities of daily living. These reasons are why individuals with substantial assets, like our mom and dad, choose to purchase long-term care insurance and create an estate plan to protect their assets. Before Dad turned 65, my parents purchased a long-term care insurance policy, understanding that they each had a parent that required nursing home care at the end of their lives. Both their parents had nursing home care covered by Medicaid because of their limited assets. Mom and Dad, however, successfully saved and planned for a secure, financially independent retirement. They knew they would not qualify for Medicaid unless they spent their substantial assets on nursing home care over several years. To mitigate the loss of those assets, they purchased long-term care insurance.

I found that my parents' daily benefit amount for coverage in an assisted living facility was set at $179/day at the outset of the policy. However, this amount increases every year in accord with annual inflation due to their purchase of the "inflation rider." The term hands-on assistance policy provision meant that coverage benefits necessitated direct hands-on care by assisted living or nursing home staff rather than "stand-by assistance." The coverage benefits in the policy are based on my parents' needing assistance with two of the six activities of daily living for policy benefits to trigger. The policy's elimination period was set at 90 days which meant when care began my parents would be responsible for paying for the first 90 days of care before the policy benefits would activate. And finally, the lifetime benefit provision in the policy means there is no limit of days or dollar amount to the benefits my parents will receive under the policy.

In contrast to my parents' lifetime coverage, I know of two friends whose parents also have long-term care insurance policies. Their policies have different criteria for the benefit period than my parents' policy. One of those policies has a lifetime maximum payout of $250,000 and the other has a two-year benefit period maximum. Those policy benefits are far inferior to the policy my parents have. A $250,000 benefit could be exhausted in as little as two years if an expensive care facility were chosen or could last quite some time if only home health care benefits were used, depending on the schedule of use. For the policy with a two-year benefit period, that family is waiting as long as possible to begin using the policy benefits, so they are less likely to have benefits expire. This approach leads to risk of falls and other problems in delaying needed assistance.

There were difficulties with Meals on Wheels deliveries and the meals provided. They received the meals for about a month, but they were routinely delivered by an acquaintance of my dad's from their church, who is about his same age. That seemed to be embarrassing to him. Also, more than once tacos were the meal they received. In those instances, the individual ingredients had to be combined into the taco shell. He and Mom did not know how to eat them or how to assemble them and were very frustrated. More than once, we suggested just eating the ingredients in a pile on the plate with the taco shell in several pieces like nacho chips. They didn't like this option, but also Mom and Dad had very strict eating timelines despite a lot of free time. The meals were not always delivered at the same time each day, although generally within a timeframe of one hour or so. They did not like that ambiguity. This was especially true for our mom, who became very frustrated and confused by it all, so discarded the idea of Meals on Wheels within weeks because of those issues.

At about this same time my sisters, Ann and Sue, and I began communicating frequently through a group chat and were much more consistent in our interactions. We used the chat to keep each other informed of what we were hearing and to share news or information gained from caregivers, doctors, and their long-term care and Medicare insurers. At times when there were big concerns and a lot to catch up on, we had evening three-way conference calls to update one another. Our communication through these mechanisms has always been productive and helpful. Most importantly, I believe that it has had a direct impact on improving care and resources for both our mom and dad.

After the Meals on Wheels failure, we again contacted the local Aging and Disability Resource Center (ADRC) to obtain a list of home care/home health providers. We found Home Instead, contacted them, and set it up for them to come to their home three days a week to start home health care for our mother. They focused on assisting Mom with meal preparation, some light house cleaning, and played memory games and put puzzles together with her. This was an attempt to reduce the dementia progression, as she enjoyed puzzles. About a year prior to moving to assisted living, Mom had stopped playing Free Cell and Solitaire on their laptop. Over the previous year, it had become increasingly difficult for her to navigate their laptop, which was very frustrating, as she enjoyed computer games.

As a side note: in April 2025 the Trump Administration implemented federal employment layoffs, including at the Department of Health and Human Services. These cuts impacted programs that support federal aging and disability services, including Meals on Wheels. It was reported by National Public Radio that at least 40% of staff received layoff notices at the Administration for Community Living. The agency funds programs that aid senior centers and "distribute 216 million meals each year to older and disabled individuals through the Meals on Wheels program."[63]

The Home Instead aids focused on taking some stress off mom on household chores. Our goal of using home health was to be an intermediary step toward getting them ready for the move to an assisted living facility. We began having Home Instead come in their home in October and used them for three months. The services they provided were covered by their long-term care insurance and applied to the long-term care 90-day elimination period for home care services. Their long-term care insurance policy had several policy provisions and requirements that apply to how their services are rendered and covered. These provisions are standard long-term care insurance policy requirements and are detailed in the table below. Mom resisted the idea of needing help from the home aide. Dad enjoyed it when the aides came as it provided the opportunity to talk and visit with someone new.

> In 2023, the median annual cost of a home health aide was more than $75,000, and a semi-private room in a nursing home cost $104,025, on average, according to Care Scout.[62]

Falls are a huge risk as individuals age and are the leading cause of injury for adults ages 65 years and older.[64] Over 14 million, or 1 in 4 older adults report falling every year.[65] My dad has fallen at least ten times in three years. Mom's fall at age 86 while in hospice care within the assisted living facility fractured her hip and lead to her death four days later. The risk of a fall was one of the primary reasons we wanted our parents and particularly my father to move into an assisted living facility.

An incident I will never forget occurred on Christmas Day, 2021 and expedited the move to assisted living. Dad had many health ailments, including sciatica in his legs, spinal stenosis, scoliosis, and a hiatal hernia, which made it difficult at times to swallow food. We had eaten lunch and some food he had eaten became blocked. He went to use the bathroom, but he didn't share that he was having difficulty. He was gone for some time, and I went to check on him. He had either fallen or laid down on the bathroom floor after being faint and was passed out. His coloring was gray, and I was very frightened for him. My sister Ann called 911. I tried to bring him around while we discussed the emergency with the dispatcher. The dispatcher directed us to see if he was choking or had food caught in his throat. I turned his head to the side and cleared food out of his mouth, and he started to respond to me. It was a scary few moments and the first responders arrived soon after and assessed him. They cleared him to stay home. But with this scare and increasing mobility concerns, as well as our mother's advancing dementia, we felt a move to assisted living with more care and oversight was becoming a pressing need.

At this point Home Instead had been coming to assist Mom three days a week for three months. Shortly after Dad's near-choking incident at Christmas, an apartment became available at an assisted living facility about seven miles away from their home. They toured the facility in early December and put their names on the waiting list for an apartment. The facility's director told us the wait could take several months, but somehow others ahead of them on the wait list passed, and we were extremely glad our parents made the leap and agreed to take the apartment in January 2022.

We had to tell Mom though that the assistance was also for Dad and not solely for her. And it was partially true, as his mobility was becoming limited, and we wanted to lessen his using the stairs to the basement. Mom did not understand why we wanted to lessen Dad's use of the stairs. Dad also had trouble understanding Mom's dementia progression and how it was made worse by her difficulty hearing.

After moving into the assisted living facility, we encouraged Mom to go to social events such as baking, crafts, putting together community puzzles, and social gatherings. But Mom had difficulty embracing the new environment and the social opportunities, due to her being hard of hearing and her dementia. She often felt dizzy and nauseous, and we were never able to successfully solve those ailments. As a result, she lay in the apartment for hours on end and was reluctant to go to meals or any other gatherings.

A secondary result of this was that dad was then also more isolated. Since Mom didn't want to go to the dining room for meals, he didn't either, which meant they both missed out on key social engagements the dining room offered residents. At times he said it felt like he was living alone because Mom was always sleeping. This was frustrating for him as it was difficult to understand how to help her or why she was so reluctant to participate.

Long-term care insurance policies provide coverage of long-term care and nursing services in multiple settings for those who meet eligibility requirements. For those with dementia or need for hands-on assistance with two or more activities of daily living. These reasons are why individuals, like our Mom and Dad with substantial assets, choose to purchase long-term care insurance and create an estate plan to protect their assets. Before Dad turned 65, they purchased a long-term care insurance policy, understanding that they each had a parent that required nursing home care at the end of their lives. Both their parents had nursing home care covered by Medicaid because of their limited assets. Mom and Dad, however, successfully saved and planned for a secure, financially independent retirement. They knew they would not qualify for Medicaid unless they had to spend their substantial assets on nursing home care over several years. To mitigate the loss of those assets, they purchased long-term care insurance.

When Mom and Dad moved into the assisted living facility, we met with care staff and determined that Dad would have assistance with two activities of daily living to ensure he would meet his long-term care policy's eligibility standard for coverage. The two ADL's we identified for assistance were bathing and transferring. Dad's shower schedule was three days each week with the aide standing by as he gets in and out of the shower. Shortly before moving into the assisted living facility Dad began using a walker and less frequently, a wheelchair. Aides would also assist Dad in getting in and out of his wheelchair and escorting him to the dining room for each meal. The dining room was a long distance from their apartment, so the wheelchair became necessary soon after the move to get to meals. At the time of their move, in 2021, the reimbursement level for their policy for care in an assisted living facility was $169/day or $5,070 per month. The inflation rider associated with their policy increases the reimbursement level for care by 5% each year. In 2025 the assisted living facility reimbursement rate is $204/day or $6,120 per month. Under Dad's policy the nursing home and memory care rate is $339/day. Currently Dad's assisted living care costs at level two are $5,567 per month so his costs are currently covered in full with nothing out-of-pocket paid by him.

Activities of Daily Living (ADL)

ADLs essentially indicate one's ability to care for themselves without assistance.

1. **Transferring:** This includes the ability to walk, sit, stand, lie down, and get up, and climb up and down stairs, both inside and outside the home.
2. **Bathing/Grooming:** This includes all activities necessary to maintain personal hygiene, like brushing teeth, bathing, shaving, and hair and nail care.
3. **Toileting:** This includes the ability to control the bladder and bowels (continence), use the toilet safely, and clean oneself after use.
4. **Continence:** The ability to control movements of the bowels and bladder.

> **5. Dressing:** The ability of an individual to dress them-
> selves, including using buttons and zippers.
> **6. Feeding:** This includes the ability to use cutlery and
> feed oneself.

Dad resisted assistance with showering as he was not comfortable with being naked in front of care staff. During the first month we emphasized with Dad that assistance was mandatory for coverage of services. He continued to resist help, and therefore, during the first month he only was assisted with one ADL. As a result, he did not meet the coverage eligibility requirement and his first month of care did not meet the elimination period eligibility, so the 90-day clock started one month late, costing them about $5,000.

When they moved into the assisted living facility, Dad was happy that one of his old bosses from his job at the Post Office lived a few doors down the hall from them. They knew others there as well, and a woman who Mom knew, Ruth, moved in after they had been there about 16 months. Mom and Dad often ate dinner with Ruth, and it was nice to have some community connections. After moving from their con-do, Mom would often say that she missed their condo, and they should have stayed another year before making the move. Mom had very little recognition of hers or Dad's needs and why they really needed to be in an assisted living environment.

A few months after they moved to assisted living, we held an estate sale at their former home. Ann priced everything and managed the sale as she was finalizing her purchase of the home and planned to move in. Our Mom and Dad came to the house prior to the sale. Mom went through everything and questioned the pricing and lamented that she wanted to keep several items. Mom wanted to reprice many items to what they would cost new rather than in their state after forty years of use. She had difficulty processing that her items were more valuable to her than as a used item to someone else. It was very difficult for her to see her cherished items for sale that did not fit in their small, assisted living apartment.

One of the extra services for residents of their assisted living facility was the use of a Lincoln Town Car and driver for getting to doctor appointments and other needs. Dad knew the driver from their church and would occasionally use the "limo" service, as he called it. But Dad still enjoyed driving and often pushed back on our suggestions to use the limo more. Every Thursday Dad and four of his buddies from high school had a planned breakfast at a local restaurant. Over time some other men joined the group, and depending on their health, most of time there were four or five men who would show up. But as their health worsened or some men passed away, the attendance diminished. One friend fell and broke his leg and was in a nursing home for some time, during which his children sold his home and car. Dad mentioned this to us frequently as he seemed worried, we might do the same, despite our legitimate concerns for an 88-year-old man driving who complained of double vision. He would tell us his remedy was to either squint or close one eye and the double vision would go away. This remedy did not alleviate our concern.

One benefit throughout Mom and Dad's stay was having occasional visits from their priest and a deacon at their church. These were sporadic, and we tried to have them be more routine as both Mom and Dad enjoyed having visitors. Mom also resisted attending social activities provided by the assisted living facility such as working with crafts or chair exercises.

Mom's dementia continued to worsen while in assisted living. It was very worrisome during the first weekend when they moved in; we saw Mom get turned around, heading down the wrong hallway rather than to her apartment. This was a huge concern because we were told if Mom was disoriented or lost within the facility, she could be moved to the Memory Care Unit.

Her primary doctor suggested a medicinal patch to treat dementia that would be placed on her upper arm daily. The Exelon patch is approved for treatment of mild to moderate dementia of the Alzheimer's type and mild to moderate dementia associated with Parkinson's disease. Up to this point my dad was managing both his own and our mom's medications. At one point Mom missed her morning medications and wanted to take all her medications for that day simultaneously later that day. Luckily, Dad mentioned this to Ann, and she was able to talk them out of doing that. This incident, combined with needing to apply the patch daily, made us decide that medication management should be reassigned to the assisted living care staff. Dad was very reluctant to let this go, in part because it meant all medications would be distributed to the assisted living facility through the assisted Living Pharmacy Service (ALPS) and would no longer be through their Medicare Part D benefit with United Health care. This change meant their combined prescription costs increased overall to about $200 per month. But given the difficulty in administering Mom's Exelon patch, we felt it was a safety concern, and she could either miss doses or end up with multiple patches on her body at the same time. Dad insisted he could manage this, but we argued that it was a safety concern of the facility, and they were there to provide this needed assistance. In their first few months residing in the assisted living facility, it was difficult to get them to buy in completely to the "assistance" aspect of their new surroundings.

There had been so many incidents within the assisted

living facility – the falls, the medication difficulties, the dizzy spells – but because these didn't occur while they were home alone, it kept both Mom and Dad safe. If those had occurred at home the consequences could have been immense.

As Mom's dementia progressed, she slept more and more. This was extremely hard on Dad, as he even commented that at times he felt as if he was living alone. She was reluctant to do anything out of fear she would become dizzy. This was very isolating for Dad who was always more outgoing and in need of conversation than Mom. Mom became uninterested in puzzles as they became difficult for her. She could no longer follow storylines of tv shows due equally to her difficulty hearing and dementia. Mom also was often frustrated with failing to understand family conversations around her and in the dining room at assisted living causing her to withdraw and become frustrated.

As Mom's dementia progressed, she started having debilitating nausea, had difficulty eating and would refuse to eat. Her lack of eating was made worse by her and my dad's reluctance to drink fluids. My sister Ann started routinely bringing them Gatorade and Pedialyte. No matter how much we encouraged fluids, Mom could not drink more than one or two ounces a day. This continued for two months or so. Eventually the lead nurse at the assisted living facility, Shannon, suggested Mom was failing to thrive, and we should consider hospice care. Shannon helped us coordinate the hospice care, which was covered in full by her Medicare Advantage plan. Shannon provided three hospice provider options that she saw as very helpful and provided quality care. Ann, Sue, and I decided to go with Shannon's highest recommendation.

The hospice staff provided Mom's care in her apartment at the assisted living facility, so the transition was very easy, and the two entities coordinated efforts seamlessly. This was, however, a confusing time for Dad, as we tried to explain that Mom's health was deteriorating. Hospice care was in place for about three weeks when one night Mom got up in the middle of the night to use the bathroom. She was very weak from the lack of nutrition, having not eaten anything substantial in the previous three weeks. On her way to the bathroom, she fell in the bedroom and broke her hip. At the emergency room she was assessed, and it was determined that she was too weak for surgery to repair her hip. Later that day she was brought back to the assisted living facility, and we resumed hospice care, making her as comfortable as possible with pain medicine. Our focus was to be with Mom every moment and make her comfortable. Hospice told us she would not survive more than two weeks as she was unable to eat anything substantial only eating ice chips. My Dad, sisters, nieces, and I were able to be with her over her final days continuously and she passed away four days after the fall and hip fracture. During this time, we were sustained and lifted up by the exceptional care provided by the hospice team. In her final days the hospice team added chaplain visits to aid us in prayer and sharing stories of Mom's impact on us all. An additional help was a booklet about hospice care and end of life process-

---

Hospice Care Explained

Hospice care is a type of compassionate care provided to individuals who are in the final stages of a terminal illness. It focuses on comfort and quality of life rather than attempting to cure the disease. The care provided includes a range of services:

- Medical support
- Pain management
- Emotional and spiritual assistance
- Location of services is flexible
- Additional support such as daily activities and bereavement support

---

es given to us by Mom's hospice nurse. It was a time of peace and grace that I will cherish. I thought I knew how amazing hospice providers were before this experience. Instead, I underestimated their lasting impact on me personally and what they provided as Mom eased into her next life.

Mom's passing was devasting to us, but it was especially hard on our dad. Dad spent 63 years with our mom by his side. They were apart for less than a week total during their entire marriage. We increased our visits and tried to have him engage in more activities in the facility. This helped a bit, and slowly, over time he made a few new friends, which helped, and he was able to eat meals in the dining room with a close group of friends.

One incredibly unique and amazing thing about Dad is his loyalty to his friends. At 86 Dad still kept in contact with more than a dozen grade school classmates and organized class reunions. He reserved a restaurant, sent invitations, and facilitated the gatherings for his 50th and 60th eighth grade class reunions. These reunions included 10-15 classmates – even into their 80s. Two of those classmates traveled from Georgia and Texas. Those two friends joined the military service at the same time as Dad, in 1954, before the Korean War ended. This allowed them to take advantage of the GI Bill. Their bond was amazingly strong. Dad's good friend, Dick, who lives in San Antonio, Texas even visited Dad in August of 2024. These reunion dinners occurred until 2020, at the local restaurant Dad selected. Mom and Dad even invited those who attended to their home afterward for cocktails and more reminiscing into the evening.

These efforts by Dad says more about him and what he meant to his friends, and in turn what they meant to him, than anything else I can share. It is an amazing measure of a man to do this for his friends and classmates 70 years from when they were in school together.

Dad also maintains enormous pride in being a mailman. He believes it is an extension of his service in the Air Force. This is perhaps a metaphor stretched too far, but I believe it with every fiber I have. Dad always delivered for his country, for his mail customers, for his friends and classmates, for his bowling team members, and for his children every day. But most of all, he was there for Mom. They were inseparable and were perfectly matched. He delivered everything she ever needed, and she did the same for Dad.

In the fall of 2024, about six months after Mom's passing, Dad's mobility noticeably deteriorated, and he fell in November and December. So, the Friday after Christmas we went scooter/motorized wheelchair shopping. Dad tried several models and that afternoon he bought a large scooter and took it to his assisted living facility. There were, however, problems, and we realized a smaller wheelchair was a better choice. The DME provider was able to switch them out a few days later. Dad steers with a joystick, and it's small enough that he can sit on the scooter while eating in the dining room.

With all of that still in place, Dad fell twice again in January of 2025. We were concerned also that he was routinely falling asleep mid-conversation when we visited in person and while talking on the phone. Because of these falls, the assisted living facility increased Dad's interaction with staff and level of care to its highest level in an assisted living environment.

The dangers our dad was dealing with were increasing in numerous ways, and we decided to look into removing his driver's license. Sue contacted the Department of Motor Vehicles and found a form which allowed each of us to fill it out confidentially and submit it to the DMV. We also gave a copy to Dad's primary care doctor, who also filled it out and submitted it to DMV. About a week later Dad received a notice in the mail that his license had been revoked, and he was no longer able to drive. The letter stated he could appeal it and take a driver's test, but he told Ann that he knew he was unlikely to pass. Dad was not nearly as upset as we feared, as he assumed his doctor was right about the safety concerns with his driving.

A result of Dad no longer driving is that Ann now takes him to all of his appointments and also often runs errands to the pharmacy and grocery store since Ann lives a few miles away. I live over two hours away and Sue is a four-hour drive away, so Ann assists with these essential activities almost exclusively verses Sue and me. After Mom passed, Ann also increased her visits to Dad as he was definitely lonelier without Mom by his side. Ann had already been taking both Mom and Dad to their appointments when she could after they had moved to assisted living. Ann's attendance at the appointments was needed because they would either forget what the doctors told them at the appointment or had forgotten entirely to ask key questions. We also realized that we should have had proxy access for both mom's and dad's electronic medical record once we had established the medical power of attorney in 2022. We received access after our request in February 2025. There was also a question about whether Dad had a Do Not Resuscitate directive on file. We thought he did since Mom had.

One other impact for Ann relates to the "sandwich generation" referenced earlier in the book. In addition to driving our mom and dad to appointments and routinely checking in on them, she also routinely provides care and helps her daughters by watching her seven grandchildren, all age eight or under.

After Mom's passing we were concerned about loneliness issues for Dad. While in assisted living, Mom had also complained about loneliness, even though she repeatedly avoided participating in the social activities offered. I was concerned about Dad's loneliness because of my history with Medicaid long-term care services and support for those who are older and/or have disabilities. I have learned a great deal through learning about how Pyx Health assists vulnerable people overcome loneliness and its inter-related problems. Pyx Health's efforts reduce loneliness and improve patient outcomes by identifying hidden risks, closing care gaps, and addressing unmet health needs. For instance, 42% of seniors in care facilities report severe loneliness compared to just 10% of those aging at home. And isolated seniors spend an extra $1,644 per year on health care, experience longer hospital stays, more frequent readmissions, and faster cognitive and physical decline.[66]

Dad's mobility continued to worsen, and he was also dealing with swollen feet that made it hard to walk and put on his orthotic shoes. The swelling was caused by his retaining water due to some new medication. During a routine office visit, his primary care physician found that he also had fluid in his lungs. At the visit his blood pressure was 196/94. Because of the high blood pressure reading and fluid retention, she was concerned he may have heart failure and directed that he be taken immediately to the emergency room. At the emergency room they were able to reduce the fluid in his lungs and change his diuretic medication to reduce fluid retention. He then had a follow up appointment for wound care related to the ankle swelling a week later. To also deal with his worsening mobility, his primary care physician suggested physical therapy to increase Dad's flexibility and strength. Physical therapy has been a benefit, and the therapist has stated he has made improvements.

Facilitating and coordinating Mom and Dad's care, managing their appointments, insurance and other needs has required all three of us children to play important roles and to communicate to each other. Sharing what they each parent told us and what we were seeing was even more vital as Mom's dementia worsened. Now with Dad living alone without Mom, it is even more essential. For some reason, at times Dad has not told me certain key things, such as the pain he was experiencing, that he was sharing more readily with Ann and Sue. This is why routine three-way conference calls and daily texting prove essential; especially as major changes occurred. At challenging times these calls have been really important for instance at the time of one of Dad's falls and subsequent ER visit. These calls also helped us make major decisions such as deciding to implement Mom's hospice care when she was refusing to eat and drink and she became weaker by the day. Even with our vigilance and communication with each other, one person has helped tremendously by communicating what she sees on the inside. Shannon, the lead nurse within the assisted living community, oversees all care staff for the 150 residents. Shannon's routine texting, phone calls, and emails to us keep us abreast of what is going on with Dad, his medication issues, and daily blood pressure readings. Without Shannon's communication, we would have much more anxiety and questions and concerns about Dad's care. I know Shannon cannot possibly provide this level of communication and support for all the facilities residents. This again speaks to Dad's personality and easy likability.

With Dad's worsening mobility and increasing falls and now complaints of dizziness, we decided to look at nursing home options. Two tours of possible options were helpful to introduce the idea of increasing Dad's level of care. He indicated he preferred one option more than the other facility we toured. This proactive effort will be helpful in case we need to make an urgent decision in the future. However, it feels like this move is likely to be needed in the near future.

Dad's steadiness worsened as time passed and one night in January, he awoke at 3:00 a.m. to use the restroom. He noticed that his six-foot-tall grandfather clock had stopped. The clock is 50 years old and needs to have the weights manually adjusted once every five days or so to keep it operating on time. The three weights are about 20 pounds each so adjusting them at 3:00 a.m. is risky. Well, on this occasion, Dad lost his balance while adjusting a weight and he says he grabbed it as he was falling backward. The weight broke and caused the clock to fall on him as he fell. Luckily, he somehow only incurred cuts and bruises on his hand; it could have been so much worse. Also, because he had his emergency call pendant on around his neck, he was able to call for assistance. The aide lifted the clock off Dad, but because the facility is assisted living, aides are not allowed to lift residents. Instead, they can only provide stand-by assistance. Dad eventually was able to get up on his own with the aide standing by. Dad's falls were progressively more dangerous and caused us to consider a move to a higher level of care facility.

Another result of this fall was Dad was upset that the facility called both Ann and I to alert us to his fall. Shannon suggested Ann take him to urgent care for an x-ray of his hand two days later. He said he felt like the facility treats him like a child. We again said to Dad that there were concerns about his safety and well-being when he falls and we need to be alerted. The x-ray, gratefully, was negative.

Two weeks after the grandfather-clock-induced fall, Dad finally had his cognitive assessment appointment with a neurologist that we had scheduled eight months earlier. Ann took Dad to both the evaluation and subsequent review of the findings. The evaluation found that Dad now has Lewy body dementia (LBD), the second most common type of dementia after Alzheimer's disease. The neurologist indicated LBD involves abnormal protein deposits called Lewy bodies in the brain. LBD affects areas of the brain involved in thinking, memory, and movement. The neurologist told Ann that symptoms may include changes in mood, vision, sleep disturbances, and cognitive fluctuations. Other effects of LBD include increases in blood pressure and bladder accidents. We have seen these symptoms increasing in the past three months or so. LBD can also cause agitation, aggressive behavior, causing a person to become combative. At a follow-up appointment a week later, the neurologist prescribed a new drug to help mitigate and slow the progression of his dementia. Dad's physician also suggested that we consider speech therapy to help improve functionality and slow deterioration of cognition.

A few months after the LBD diagnosis, Dad had two medical emergencies within three weeks of each other. The first involved an emergency room visit when he was found unresponsive sitting outside in the sun on a hot afternoon. Luckily, Shannon happened to be outside in front of the facility that day and went to say hello to Dad. He was unresponsive, and she could not detect a pulse, so she called for an ambulance. Dad was assessed and taken to the nearest hospital and emergency medical technicians administered Narcan in route as he was still unresponsive. Because they saw that Dad was prescribed a controlled substance for his pain, the Narcan was an option. He regained consciousness and was given IV fluids and a chest x-ray. Ann took him back to the assisted living facility that evening and the cause was labeled as dehydration. Dad sips water off and on during the day but rarely drinks more than eight ounces a day based on our estimates. We routinely emphasize the need to hydrate, and he claims to drink much more. He is reluctant to drink more due to his incontinence.

The second incident occurred when he was getting ready for his shower with care staff in his apartment. He was undressing while sitting on the toilet and became unresponsive. The aide called for help and got him to his bed, and the lead nurse came as he regained consciousness. She assisted in making him comfortable and hydrated as Ann arrived. Ann stayed with Dad for several hours while he slowly began to feel better.

After these incidents we realized bringing Dad via the ambulance to the ER to receive IV fluids was not a helpful long-term solution. We began to think about a move to another nursing facility that could provide more hands-on care. But we also did not want to disrupt his routine and have a dramatic change in environment. It was suggested that perhaps hospice could be started to provide more intensive attention to his needs and avoid ER visits. A hospice assessment was completed, and Dad was approved. Hospice staff now see Dad three times per week and provide care that is focused on making him comfortable. Dad is considered to be in congestive heart failure, although his high blood pressure has been under better control of late with improved timing of his medications. The additional monitoring and support by the hospice staff in the initial month has helped. An oxygen tank is also now available for use by Hospice in his apartment. Dad continues to have very swollen feet, indicating functionality problems with his heart and kidneys, and he still has bouts of dizziness. We're hopeful that hospice will continue to help Dad stabilize and lessen the dizziness, avoid dehydration and ER visits, and in general make him as comfortable as possible.

Dad continued to decline during the fall of 2025, and hospice being involved was very helpful. Dad's LBD hallucinations became more frequent, and his speech became more garbled. He discussed his upcoming 90th birthday frequently and reminisced about key moments in his life. Dad enjoyed his 90th birthday party with many friends and family sharing in the celebration at the assisted living facility. With his pain increasing, Dad was becoming less steady standing and using his walker. A week after the party Dad fell twice within the space of about six hours. After the first fall, an aid found him fully dressed lying on the floor of his living room and called Ann at about 1:00 a.m. The aid explained that Dad was not hurt but was disoriented and got him back into bed, then gave him more lorazepam and morphine.

Then Dad fell again at about 7:00 a.m. and was very confused, not making sense, but again was not physically hurt. Hospice was called and evaluated him an hour or so later. Dad was hallucinating and agitated, saying there were 15 children running around his apartment. Shannon, the lead nurse, was able to join Ann, Sue, and I on a conference call and she suggested this could be a major change in Dad's status. Sue and I arrived early that afternoon and continued to stay with him over the next five days. That day Dad continued to slowly decline, and over the next day or so he only had a few hours of effective interaction with us. Hospice decided to increase Dad's lorazepam and morphine to reduce the hallucinations and agitation, making Dad more comfortable.

Three days before he passed away his hallucinations and interaction with us lessened, though his agitation and heavy breathing was still occurring. Another increase in lorazepam and morphine reduced restlessness, and he became more peaceful. Over those last five days we were there with Dad continuously. We said our goodbyes as he passed away on Sunday night, December 14th, joining Mom in heaven. The funeral was held the day after Christmas with Dad surrounded by friends and family celebrating a remarkable man. Dad's was the definition of a life well-lived – a man of integrity and dedication to his family.

Summary

Throughout the care of our parents, Ann, Sue, and I have learned so much and worked through some frustrating, confusing, and very sad times. Sue routinely comments about how complex and challenging managing our parents' long-term care issues has been. It is stressful and frustrating as the roles reverse and we take care and oversight of our parents' needs. That transition of roles is not easy on parents either, as they feel a loss of control, autonomy, and privacy. As stated earlier, having routine insights from Shannon, the lead nurse at the assisted living facility, had been a godsend. But most importantly effective, routine communication among the three of us children without drama, ego, or avoidance helped more than I can ever say. It takes an enormous amount of effort, especially by Ann who has had to transport Mom and Dad to so many appointments and answer too many alarming 3:00 a.m. phone calls. There is nothing easy about managing long-term care needs, but our constant communication among the three of us has helped us and our parents immensely through this challenging journey.

Aging and Disability Resource Centers (ADRCs)

Taking a quick step back, an important resource now widely available to US citizens are ADRCs, which are available in all states. CMS first awarded ADRC grants to 12 states in 2003. Each year the number of states participating in the program grew, and now all states and several territories receive funding to develop ADRC Programs. ADRCs seek to address the frustrations many older adults, people with disabilities, and family members experience when trying to learn about and access long-term services and supports. ADRC's are an amazing resource and connection point to essential services.

ADRCs raise visibility about the full range of available options; provide objective information, advice, counseling, and assistance; empower people to make informed decisions about their long-term services and supports; and help people access public and private programs. ADRCs provide unbiased, reliable information and counseling to people with all levels of income.

According to their website, ADRCs are an important part of the No Wrong Door (NWD) system model. NWD is a collaboration between the Administration for Community Living (ACL), the Centers for Medicare & Medicaid Services (CMS), and the Veterans Health Administration. The NWD initiative supports states working to streamline access to long-term services and supports for older adults, people with disabilities, and their families.

Journey 2

Jay and His Mid-Career Stroke, Causing Disability

Jay is 52 years old, husband to Lori and father to two teenage boys. He served in the Air Force for ten years as an A-10 Warhawk pilot stationed in Tucson, Arizona, Germany, and South Korea. He retired in 2009 as a Major-Select, and his primary duties included instructing other pilots. Jay had earned a business degree after his service with the use of the GI Bill. After graduation he decided to use that business experience and his gift of communication and leadership experience to become a marketing professional. Jay's life dramatically changed at age 51 while working as Director of Marketing and Communications for a large religious organization in Milwaukee, Wisconsin. This event occurred at the outset of the COVID-19 public health pandemic in March 2020. Jay had a severe arteriovenous malformation (AVM) that ruptured, causing a hemorrhage and bleeding in his brain. Jay was immediately rushed to the emergency room, and the bleeding would not stop.

In Jay's case the AVM rupture caused a stroke. Jay spent two weeks in the hospital, including several days in intensive care, followed by three weeks in a rehabilitation facility. Jay has undergone months of speech, physical, and occupational therapy. Throughout his recovery Jay has had ups and downs, good days and bad and has seen his recovery plateau with minimal gains.

Immediately after the stroke, the initial assessment and prognosis suggested that Jay may not breathe on his own again. Five days after the stroke, Jay came out of a coma and began breathing on his own. Soon after, however, Jay had a setback, and a tracheotomy and brain shunt were needed. Doctors were able to lessen the brain swelling, which could have damaged Jay's brain stem and caused his death if swelling had continued. Long-term effects included impact on Jay's speech, making connections within conversations, and maintaining effective flow of thoughts. The stroke impacted the left side of Jay's brain causing nerve damage on his right side.

Due to COVID-19, Lori could not see Jay while he was in the hospital or in the rehabilitation facility for six weeks, so she continued to teach at her school via Zoom. The boys were also in school via Zoom virtually and missed their father tremendously. During this six-week period they could only see him through a hospital room window and could not interact directly.

When released from the hospital, much of Jay's recovery, therapy, and care occurred at home, which was difficult as well for the boys to see. The boys were deeply impacted by Jay's stroke and recovery and both participated in therapy. Lori said one son also needed emergency therapy at one point because it was so traumatic for him.

COVID-19 also made it very difficult for Jay to participate in stroke and aphasia support groups, depriving him of valuable community and peer support. But one helpful benefit through the University of Wisconsin is his receipt of therapy from students in its Master's in Speech Therapy program. The therapy is inexpensive because it is provided by students, even though Jay receives the latest techniques in therapy being taught the students.

Jay and Lori met while he was serving in the Air Force

in Korea. At the time Lori was a teacher at a Department of Defense school for children of military personnel. The two met and hit it off at a "Come as You Were in High School" party, despite Jay wearing Birkenstocks and a tie dye t-shirt, Lori joked. They were married about two years later despite being separated much of that time after Lori returned home to Ohio where she grew up. Lori found Jay to be a confident, engaging man with a great sense of humor. They then reunited in Tucson, Arizona when Jay was transferred to a base there and were married in 2005. They have two teenage boys who were 13 and ten at the time of Jay's stroke. The eldest is now starting college in 2025.

Soon after I first met Jay in 2013 through Lori's brother Marty, a Chick-Fil-A restaurant opened its first location near my home. It turned out both Jay and I quickly became big fans of the restaurant chain. In the next few months, I saw him there, either with his boys or with Lori, or the whole family, at least five times. It was so often it became a running joke whenever I saw my good friend Marty. Marty and his wife Jessica are good friends of mine and would always ask if I had seen Jay at Chick-Fil-A recently. It was humorous because the answer was always 'yes.' But the most fun remembrance was playing Cards Against Humanity with Jay and Lori and others in that first encounter at Marty and Jessica's house. This first time meeting them occurred shortly after they had moved from Tucson to Wisconsin in 2013. Jay was the life of that party and the party's still are livelier whenever he's involved.

Lori is a first-grade teacher at a public school near their home. Immediately after the stroke occurred, a substitute teacher temporarily took over Lori's first grade class. Lori was able to take some family medical leave to keep her job and care for Jay when he returned home after his rehabilitation facility stay.

Jay's health insurance coverage shifted to coverage under Lori's employer several months after the stroke because his employment ended. About a year after Jay's stroke their coverage was transitioned to a different insurer. Lynn had to locate a different primary care physician for Jay, but luckily, Jay's neurologist was contracted with both insurers, allowing seamless and continuous care. With military benefits and health insurance coverage through Lynn's employer, Jay's insurance coverage became even more complicated with his approval for Social Security disability. With this approval, Jay became eligible for Medicaid but then was also eligible for Medicare after the mandatory 24-month waiting period.

Jay's employment benefits included health insurance and both short and long-term disability insurance coverage. Jay's health insurance covered his emergency surgery, inpatient hospital stay, and rehabilitation facility stay. Because some of Jay's health coverage is covered by the VA, his electronic medical records are in multiple systems and not shared among all providers like they should be. In this era of technology, the VA is not as advanced as the majority of the health care industry in sharing and providing a complete medical record for its military patients.

Jay does receive most of his health care services at the VA, including his primary care, speech and physical therapy, vision services, annual exams, and acupuncture. Lori calls Jay's use of VA

> **VA PIRATE Program**[67]
> Treatment through PIRATE can help individuals with aphasia improve their listening, speaking, reading, or writing abilities and may include the use of communication technology.
>
> PIRATE is offered throughout the year, with a maximum of six sessions per year. Each session is 4 weeks long, and therapy takes place on weekdays, during business hours. Patients' family members can participate in select educational and therapy sessions.

health services a "huge blessing." Jay does walk with a very slight limp, but most of the impact of the stroke is on his speech due to aphasia. Aphasia is defined as a comprehension and communication (reading, speaking, or writing) disorder resulting from damage or injury to the specific area in the brain that is associated with those functions. Jay receives reading therapy with two different therapists four days per week. Jay's most significant struggles are with writing and reading. Jay's reading comprehension is challenging, with impacts on his executive decision-making and functioning. Jay is concentrating on to-do lists and scheduling tasks as a means to address the challenges. At the VA Jay also receives acupuncture, massage therapy, and contrast therapy, which alternates hot and cold to promote healing, reduce pain, and enhance overall wellness.

Before his stroke, Jay was a Director of Marketing and Community Engagement, with responsibilities across several counties. Jay's sense of humor and outgoing nature were useful attributes in his daily work. Jay's colleagues and community partner agency contacts were stunned by the stroke with numerous contacts stepping up to aid Lori and the family with support of meals and other assistance.

To remain engaged with some work-oriented activities, Jay now attends staff meetings, though he is not actively employed. In addition, Jay is a youth and religious confirmation volunteer with his church community.

Jay's VA speech therapist suggested that an aphasia program in Pittsburgh might be helpful for him. The Pittsburgh area VA's Program for Intensive Residential Aphasia Treatment and Education (PIRATE) provides treatment to veterans and active-duty service members with aphasia without a fee. Jay participated in the program twice, spending three weeks at the Pittsburgh VA each time. Jay participated once as a student in the program and then also within a clinical trial, testing a live functional MRI while Jay completed tasks to identify the impact of treatment for his aphasia. By providing education and support, patients and families begin to understand that their diagnosis and deficits are multifaceted, and recovery is an ongoing process.

In Jay's day-to-day job, effective communication was paramount in speaking to community groups and in his written marketing efforts. Communication and getting his point across correctly is a struggle for Jay now. He knows what he wants to say but getting that across from brain to verbalization is where the breakdown occurs.

Lori and Jay applied for and received approval from the Social Security Administration to attain disability benefits for Jay. This disability application process was arduous and confusing, but Lori had assistance from Jay's employer's disability insurer in understanding the process. She did not hire a law firm but felt that would have made the process easier. Now that the application is approved and Jay is receiving SSDI, he also has both Medicare and Medicaid coverage which are secondary to the employer-based coverage from Lori's employer. Medicaid is always the payer of

> **Social Security Disability Insurance (SSDI)**
> A federal program that pays monthly, tax-free benefits to people who cannot work because of a qualifying disability. It is available to workers who have earned enough work credits to be insured through the program. To receive SSDI, individuals must submit a disability application to the Social Security Administration, or SSA. If approved, the amount received will be based on their earnings.

last resort compared to the other coverages. Again, it cannot be overstated how complex this puzzle is to manage for Lori. Lori stated that because of disability and social security fraud in the US, application reviews assume that applicants are trying to game the system. Because of this circumspection, reviewers scrutinize all aspects and assume denial rather than approval.

Just one year prior to Jay's stroke, his employer established this disability coverage for employees. However, the initial payment of the disability benefit was delayed for a few months and Lori indicated that almost $40,000 was deposited retroactively into their bank account. Lori had difficulty getting answers on how to sort things out when she had to pay back the principal ($9,000) to the disability insurance company. She did not realize that that would be required, and it was a huge burden, including the "insane" paperwork to address the issue. The benefit was provided on a pre-tax basis, unbeknownst to Lori, causing a financial burden when filing their taxes. In addition, Lori also had to apply for disability benefits to help support their sons. Dealing with this was an added challenge and frustration with everything else Lori was dealing with in filling Jay's role for the boys as well as her own. This was all in addition to maintaining her work as a teacher and managing Jay's complex care.

Other financial challenges Lori had to navigate included tax implications. Lori is now paying the taxes quarterly to ensure they are paying correctly and not getting behind. These financial complexities were also difficult because Jay had managed the family's finances prior to the stroke.

Moving forward, Lori and Jay are looking into work options with the help of a Veteran's Affairs social worker and his local ADRC, as Jay is still just 55 years old. As discussed in the Medicaid chapter earlier, he can also seek to enroll in MAPP, Wisconsin's Medicaid buy-in program and utilize the available work incentives. These are viable options for Jay if he chooses to work or volunteer or if he is required to do so under the new

OBBBA work requirements. MAPP is one of many programs Jay can seek to use by discussing them with either his Veteran's Affairs contacts or his county ADRC. Benefits counseling is another means that people with disabilities can use to assess how work may impact their Medicaid coverage and benefits eligibility. The ADRC can facilitate and recommend programs and resources, such as benefits counseling, to assist Jay. The OBBBA newly enacted work requirements discussed earlier in the Medicaid chapter may impact Jay if he is deemed to not be medically or mentally exempt. It is also important in assessing Medicaid options to consult an estate law attorney for the family's financial stability, ensuring decisions take into account the future of Lori and Jay's children as well.

His employer has become a means for Jay to keep engaged with the faith community, keep social relationships, and find a means to make valuable contributions. At this point Jay is working five hours per week at his employer's offices and stays under what is termed substantial gainful activity (SGA) to not jeopardize his Social Security Disability Insurance (SSDI) benefit. SGA refers to the level of work activity that can affect eligibility for SSDI. SGA serves as a threshold to evaluate whether a person with a disability can engage in substantial work despite their condition. In 2026 the SGA limit is $1,690 per month ($2,830 if the individual is blind). If an individual earns above this amount, they are generally considered to be engaging in SGA, which may disqualify them from receiving disability benefits. This will be a consideration if Jay considers returning to work at a substantial level. Benefits counseling can assist in helping Jay and Lori determine the level of his work effort and the implications upon his social security benefits.

Jay's long-term prognosis is still an open question. Most medical gains by people with a stroke and AVM are made in the first twelve months. Small, incremental gains can be made, but my research and Lori's statements regarding aphasia indicate large gains are unlikely for Jay moving forward.

Summary

Lori's advocacy on behalf of Jay is relentless and inspiring as she continually looks for new ways to improve his daily services and finding new ways to advance his care and healing. She has traveled to Pittsburgh numerous times while he stayed there two different times for three-week stays. Jay's mixture of VA benefits, Medicaid and Medicare is as complex as it gets as he strives to engage more with his community through volunteering and possibly re-engaging in work. Lori's continual effort to uncover new benefits and programming to enhance Jay's quality of life is inspiring. Lori questions what else is possible, what more she can do. Her tenacious advocacy for Jay is my biggest takeaway of their story.

Jay's progress since his initial hospital stay following the stroke amid COVID-19 when it was felt he may not breathe again on his own, has been remarkable though has plateaued. In the end Jay's personality and humor are still very evident and are his calling card as he always finds a way to engage and share a smile. The most recent time I met with Lori and Jay, he reminded me that he still enjoys Chick Fil-A.

Journey 3

Aaron – Adult Male with Severe Down Syndrome Since Birth

Aaron, aged 52, has Down syndrome and intellectual disabilities. At birth Aaron needed a blood transfusion and nearly died because of oxygen deprivation. When Aaron was born, his parents were older – his father, Ron, was 40 and his mother, JoAnn, was 38 years of age. Aaron's IQ is estimated at about 60-70.

As a child at home, Aaron was difficult to care for, and it was difficult to understand his needs. Aaron has needed close and extensive care all of his life. Bill is Aaron's older brother by four years and remembers Aaron not learning to walk until he was three years old. Aaron did not talk at all until after age three either. Ron and JoAnn lived 20 or so miles north of Green Bay, Wisconsin after they were married and have remained in the same home for more than 60 years.

Aaron can express very little vocally but does understand more than he can express and uses simple sign language. Aaron has been classified as having a severe intellectual disability based on the following criteria:

- significant challenges in cognitive functioning and adaptive behavior
- limited understanding of written language and mathematical concepts

- ability to learn simple daily routines and respond to simple directions
- limited or no speech and reliance on nonverbal communication and gestures

Aaron's care is covered entirely by Medicaid and is managed by a county case manager in Ron and JoAnn's county of residence. Unlike Jay's journey, Aaron's health coverage is solely through one source – Medicaid – and thus not nearly as complex as Jay's health care puzzle. However, staying on top of Aaron's care has proved to be difficult, as Bill tries to learn from his mom and Aaron's caregivers how the state system works as well as in communicating with the county case manager. It seems that JoAnn has had difficulty understanding and navigating Aaron's care and how the county manages it. As Ron and JoAnn aged into their 80s, Bill became more involved and has become the lead contact for the county case manager. JoAnn does maintain involvement, however, even as she approaches 90 years of age.

Because they felt they were unable to meet Aaron's needs, Ron and JoAnn decided to have Aaron attend school at Central Wisconsin Center in Madison, a facility nearly three hours away. He began at CWC at age seven until he was ten years old. This was difficult on the family, and when Aaron was ten, it was decided that he would return home and attend Sybil Hopp School in De Pere. Sybil Hopp specifically educates children with intellectual disabilities and is about 40 minutes from the family's home. He rode the bus to and from the school. Because of his severe intellectual disabilities, Aaron never attended traditional schools or enjoyed an integrated learning setting. Until the late 1970s, children with disabilities were not educated in integrated settings. Instead, these children were separated out in schools specifically geared to those with disabilities without the benefit of integrating with healthy children their age. Today children with intellectual disabilities are often integrated in community public and private schools. In 1975 Congress passed the Education for All Handicapped Children Act, which would be reauthorized in 1990 as the Individuals with Disabilities Education Act. These laws implemented the requirement for schools to provide equal access to education for all students with disabilities. The legislation required that the federal government would supplement state funding for the costs.

While in his teens, Aaron was moved to a large care facility called Southern Wisconsin Center (SWC), which is run by the state's Department of Services in Union Grove. He resided there until 1995 when the center no longer allowed long-term residency. This was an effort to have people with intellectual disabilities, such as Aaron, reside in the community, rather than in an institutional setting. Southern Wisconsin Center is a large facility and housed over 100 patients during Aaron's stay there. SWC serves adult clients with intellectual disabilities combined with other physical or mental health disorders. The center's goal is to assist and prepare adults with disabilities to successfully live in the setting that best meets their needs, preferably in a community setting. SWC is one of three centers for individuals with intellectual disabilities managed by the Wisconsin Department of Health Services. Aaron's parents visited him every other weekend while he resided at SWC as it was more than a three-hour drive from home.

Aaron is able to repeat some words but largely communicates with limited signing. Aaron is incontinent and wears a diaper full-time and needs daily assistance with diapering and bathing, though he can dress himself. He receives assistance with showers from the care staff. He feeds himself, but all his meals are prepared by care staff.

Aaron, as an adult, has moved numerous times to different residential care facilities. After living at SWC Aaron moved to Wisconsin Rapids, but that Adult Family Home (AFH) closed down after a short time without notice. In fact, on JoAnn's last visit, she arrived at the home on a Sunday and found out Aaron was moving the next day to a home in Shawano. Bill is unsure how these care location decisions were made.

A few years ago, when Aaron was 48 years old, he had major dental issues, resulting in several extractions and crowns on several teeth. The procedures required treatment while he was sedated at Marshfield Clinic, which provides dental services for people with disabilities who have Medicaid benefits. People with Down syndrome such as Aaron often have smaller jaws and teeth, making it more difficult to practice good oral hygiene. This genetic disposition, coupled with the physical difficulty a person with Down syndrome has in brushing their teeth and their decreased immunity leads to increased incidences of gum disease and tooth decay. These combined genetic and environmental factors result in worsened oral health and greater need for treatment while under sedation.

Aaron is now residing in a small, two-bed, community-based residential facility in Oshkosh. The home is always staffed by two caretakers, except during overnight hours. Aaron's caretakers are from Senegal and Gambia and do not have strong English usage. Bill has said that despite the language barrier, communication has been good with the family. Bill says that Aaron seems to be happiest in this location, compared to all the others where he has resided. The care staff in Oshkosh have, on a few occasions, brought Aaron to Bill's house in the Green Bay area. This is far easier for Bill and JoAnn rather than traveling to Oshkosh for each visit. Over the course of time, it is clear Aaron prefers male caretakers, as he has occasionally pushed female aides and his mother, but has never done so with men.

Aaron is allergic to gluten and is lactose intolerant, making his daily diet difficult to manage for home care staff, causing Aaron digestive difficulties. Home care staff take Aaron to the local YMCA weekly to walk around the track and enjoy some community interaction.

Aaron is on three medications and recently had the dosage of one of the meds increased to lessen his physicality toward his care attendants, with spitting, pushing, hitting, and grabbing. Aaron at times has also harmed himself – hitting himself in his chin or scratching himself. Adjustments in dosages have been made at times throughout Aaron's life to manage his physicality with caregivers. The recent adjustment has helped keep Aaron on a more even temperament, according to the care staff. Bill has said the change has been helpful and luckily hasn't impacted Aaron's demeanor and alertness when he sees him.

While residing in a AFH in Shawano, Bill indicated that it seemed that Aaron may have been over-medicated at times. With Aaron it can be difficult to tell what the same baseline is, especially being on medications for 40+ years through multiple locations. While in Shawano, care staff stole Aaron's discretionary funding rather than using the funds for his benefit. Since residing in Oshkosh, Bill has had several questions from staff regarding how he'd like those discretionary funds used for Aaron. The Oshkosh staff have bought Aaron a recliner for his room and new clothes. Bill and his mother never had these questions from the Shawano home staff and wonder how much of Aaron's money was taken.

The Shawano County social worker managing Aaron's case has asked Bill and his mother if they would be interested in the county taking over guardianship of Aaron. Bill and his mother have refused. Guardians make major health and financial decisions for people with disabilities. If Bill and JoAnn were to agree with the county becoming Aaron's guardian, it would need to be approved by and subject to oversight by the courts.

When Bill and JoAnn see Aaron, he does recognize them. In the past he enjoyed going to Culver's restaurant, but at times he becomes difficult and doesn't want to leave. Generally, his days are spent watching a lot of TV, and he likes listening to music, including Little Richard. Bill says that listening to music became too much to deal with in public with Aaron's physicality. However, Aaron did attend Ron's funeral during COVID in 2022, though Bill indicated it was difficult to know if he understood that his dad had passed away.

Managing Aaron's care over the course of 50+ years has been at times very frustrating. It has been difficult to deal with confusing Medicaid rules and facility requirements. In the early years it was especially difficult without many resources available to families in the 1970s. Resources for families have improved through such organizations as ADRCs and non-profit organizations like the Down syndrome Association of Wisconsin. But for Ron and JoAnn they say it was very challenging when Aaron was young, and they often felt

> **Special Needs Trust**
> A special needs trust (SNT) can be used to protect a person with a disability's assets while also ensuring they remain eligible for public benefits like Medicaid. These trusts allow the beneficiary to have additional resources beyond what they can otherwise have and use those resources to improve their quality of life without jeopardizing their eligibility for benefits. Funds in a SNT are not counted for SSI and Medicaid programs. To establish an SNT requires consultation with financial and legal professionals.

helpless, especially when Aaron was not at home for many years as a young child. Bill says it seems there are always surprises when they visit Aaron, surprises that they should have been notified of but were not.

About twenty years ago Ron purchased a life insurance policy specific on himself that named Aaron as sole beneficiary so that when Ron passed away, Aaron would have proceeds to cover his own funeral and other expenses within their estate trust. Ron and JoAnn's estate is currently equally divided between Bill and Aaron. Bill worked on convincing JoAnn to change this with the help of his parents' estate law attorney. If JoAnn were to pass away while the estate inheritance is shared equally, Aaron's half would make him ineligible for all the care and services he currently receives, including Medicaid itself, and he would become a private pay user. Aaron's care would then be paid by his inherited funds until he spends down enough to resume eligibility for Medicaid. This means he essentially loses any value of the inheritance, and the state garners the savings by not funding Aaron's care for that period of time. In addition, becoming a private pay individual means that all of his care would be managed by Bill rather than county case workers or staff at the CBRF in which he resides. Because Aaron has no real needs beyond his care provided by the state and the very limited social security disability benefit he receives, this is an essential question to address to ensure he continues to have Medicaid eligibility.

An alternative, other than setting aside funds in a funeral trust, would be to establish a special needs trust available to assure resources for people with disabilities.

While in Oshkosh Aaron developed a blood clot in his leg, but it was successfully treated with medication. He has no other major health issues, unlike many adults his age with severe Down syndrome. He does however get lots of respiratory infections and has had COVID once in 2021.

In early 2024 Joann's will was updated to assure that Aaron's half of her estate would be held in a trust for Aaron so that he would not suddenly inherit money that would make him ineligible for Medicaid. However, I was not sure why those funds are held in a trust, because any use of them by Aaron makes him ineligible for Medicaid given the strict $2,000 asset limit. I advised Bill to seek clarification from the estate plan attorney on why the inheritance was split evenly between Bill and Aaron. Bill needed to have the assurance that provisions had been made, taking into account Aaron's disability and his inability to use any substantial inheritance.

Bill and JoAnn met with the estate law attorney, who shared the specific language with them to alleviate their concerns. Key provisions of the family's Trust state the following:

- Exempt Trust: "Aaron ("Beneficiary") has a disability which is expected to continue for life and substantially impairs him from adequately providing for his own care and support, and thus constitutes a substantial disability. This Trust is intended to be a "Qualified Disability Trust" under Section 642(b)(2)(c)of the Code and 42 USC Section 1396p(c)(2)(B)(iv) and also is intended to qualify under Section 701.0503 (3)Wis Stats. As a trust established for the benefit of an individual with a disability and therefore is exempt from claims for public support."
- "The Trustee (Bill) may amend the Trust to ensure continuing eligibility, or to secure eligibility, of the Beneficiary of Public Benefits programs to which the Beneficiary may be entitle."

So Bill, as the Trustee, can amend the Trust as necessary

to ensure Aaron maintains eligibility for Medicaid and the care he needs.

By providing this specific language to Bill, which he had not previously seen, the estate law attorney clarified Aaron's public benefit protections within the trust. In addition, the added protection of Bill as the Trustee, being able to amend the trust language to protect Aaron's public benefit eligibility, is an important safeguard. This meeting provided tremendous peace of mind for Bill, assuring that Aaron's care under Medicaid and his continued eligibility are secure.

Summary

In my conversations with Bill about Aaron's circumstances throughout our 35-year friendship, confusion and frustration about Aaron's care have been primary issues. Aaron's complex condition, confusing benefits, care management, facility changes, and poor communication by the county social workers and care providers have been very difficult for Aaron's family. In addition, confusion about the language in the trust concerning Aaron's inheritance was a concern for Bill and JoAnn. I have suggested that Bill learn as much as possible about Aaron's care and benefits to help ensure Aaron's needs are met as Bill transitions to Aaron's guardian in the future. More consistent interaction by Bill with county case managers will help his understanding of Aaron's future needs and how to manage them. It is clear that the implications of their estate plan decisions needed better communication from their attorney. But with those questions answered, Bill is now well-positioned to successfully transition to being more involved in Aaron's care. This will help Bill in the inevitable transition to being the dedicated point of contact for Aaron's care.

Journey 4

Cassie – Young Woman with Autism Spectrum Disorder Diagnosis

Cassie is a 22-year-old young woman diagnosed with Asperger's, a high-functioning disorder on the Autism spectrum. Cassie also is nearly blind without prescription eyewear. She works eight hours per week at a fast-food restaurant in her small town in Northeast Wisconsin. She was born to a young woman named Becky, who struggled with drug abuse most of her adult life. Cassie was not diagnosed with Asperger's until age 21 and struggled mightily through school for multiple reasons, including difficulty in social settings and making new friends.

When Cassie was in eighth grade and had just turned age 14, she had missed more days of school than she attended at that point in January. On this particular day, a school counselor saw that she had come to school again without bathing. The counselor asked her what was going on at home, and Cassie replied that her mother had not been home in a few days and that she had barely eaten. The counselor called the county's Child Protective Services (CPS), explaining that Cassie had missed dozens of days of school, was unkept, and struggling. CPS was unable to reach Becky and a quick interview with Cassie at the school was scheduled by CPS. Cassie gave CPS her dad's name, and they looked at court records showing he had divorced Becky ten years earlier. CPS attempted to contact

134

Mark and spoke with his new wife, Lisa. Cassie's father, Mark, and Lisa had been married four years at the time when CPS called and lived about 30 miles from Becky's apartment in an adjacent county.

Mark was unavailable due to his work that day, and Lisa was asked to meet with CPS at their office where they had taken Cassie after school. In meeting with Lisa, and having no luck in reaching Becky, CPS determined that Lisa and Mark should temporarily take Cassie into their home. Lisa stepped up, and Cassie was removed from Becky's home that day on a temporary basis.

Lisa's interaction with Cassie to this point had been very infrequent as Mark did not have regular contact with Cassie. This lack of a relationship between Mark and Cassie was the fault of both Mark and Becky. Mark was not an active father in Cassie's life and Becky's drug problems kept her from effectively parenting Cassie and interacting with Mark.

Beginning that day at the CPS office, Lisa stepped into the void and took responsibility for Cassie. This was difficult for Lisa because she had a lot on her plate as she and Mark also had an infant daughter of their own, one-year-old Lily. When Cassie came to live with them, Lisa worked full-time as an office manager at a local manufacturer while Mark worked in construction. The couple also have support from Lisa's mother, Amy, who lives ten or so miles away while also providing frequent daycare for Lily.

On that first day, Lisa brought Cassie home, while Amy picked up little Lily at daycare. Lisa provided a warm meal to Cassie, which she had been sorely missing for some time with Becky. That evening Lisa took Cassie shopping for new shoes, as her current pair were a size too small. Lisa purchased new clothes and attempted to fix Cassie's matted, messy hair. The next day, Lisa was able to facilitate Cassie's first haircut in over a year.

Cassie had new clothes, a haircut, and was bathed for her return to school the next week at a new school in Mark and Lisa's community. With all the other changes in Cassie's life, this was one more difficult change. Changes were never easy for Cassie as her mom never provided stability. Likewise, interaction between Mark, Lisa, and Cassie was difficult, and it took time to establish trust. Cassie stayed in her new bedroom nearly all the time. Cassie did not like interacting with baby Lily at all and easily became frustrated with Lily's crying. Cassie did not have an easy time creating relationships with adults because of her fear of abandonment. Making friends at school was impossible because of her lack of attendance, lack of routine bathing, and unkept appearance. Rather than establishing friendships, Cassie was often picked on and bullied.

A court hearing was held a month later to review the case and Cassie's placement. In the meantime, Becky was facing a separate court hearing related to a shoplifting charge. The charge also included possession of drugs at the time she was apprehended. The result of the court hearing on placement for Cassie resulted in 100% placement with Mark and Lisa. The order created a scheduled six-month review for Becky to assess her progress in treatment and her progress with creating a stable home environment for herself, in hopes that Cassie could stay with her on occasion.

When a child is removed from a parent's home, CPS looks for kinship care opportunities. A movement has evolved in child welfare to emphasize finding family rather than strangers to provide care in difficult times of transition for children in need. That movement, Family Finding, is the act of looking for relatives and fictive kin (individuals who are not related by blood or marriage but are considered family members due to their strong, chosen bond) of children in or at risk of entering foster care. The goal is to find and nurture healthy adult relationships for a child and identify placement opportunities where the child feels safe and loved.

As Cassie entered counseling and visited the doctor, it was determined that she struggled in school due in part to being nearly blind. She did wear glasses, but the prescription was at least three years old, and she could not clearly see the chalkboard or anything her teachers were presenting. Cassie particularly struggles in math with very limited ability to understand money, making change, and fractions.

It became clear that guidance counselors and teachers in Cassie's original school district failed her at every turn. Through most of her schooling, Cassie missed more days of school than she attended, with no assessment of her or her family's needs or struggles. If the school attempted outreach to Becky, it failed, and they eventually gave up. Despite rampant tardiness and failing to fulfill basic schoolwork and testing, Cassie was passed every year and completed junior high on schedule. When she reached high school and under Lisa's care and advocacy, Cassie finally had assistance. The high school helped determine that she needed new glasses, improved guidance counseling, and an Individualized Education Plan (IEP). All these factors aided Cassie in gaining her footing, but most importantly, she was finally attending school regularly because of Lisa. The fact that Cassie saw that this school was providing support when others gave up also made a real difference.

Lisa struggled with managing the need to work, caring for Lily, and managing Cassie's needs. During most of their marriage, Lisa received no assistance in childcare from Mark, even for Cassie, to whom Lisa has no direct genetic tie.

Mark had difficulty maintaining permanent work, creating more stress in their marriage, in addition to his lack of focus on child rearing. They divorced in early 2024. All parenting thus fell to Lisa for both Cassie and Lily. For the next year Mark had just sporadic interactions with Lily and Cassie, often not showing up for scheduled visits.

During her senior year of high school, Cassie began working four-hour shifts per week at a local fast-food restaurant. Cassie was not interested in planning her future after high school, and she was content with continuing to work at the restaurant. She continues to work eight hours per week and either walks or rides her bike to work. Cassie also helps out Lisa with watching Lily on occasion.

Cassie, for a period of time, had Foodshare benefits through the state of Wisconsin and receives coverage through enrollment in BadgerCare – an extension of Medicaid health benefits that she is eligible for due to her very limited income. Cassie became ineligible when she misreported Lisa's income by mistake and therefore lost benefits for a short period. Wisconsin FoodShare, also known as SNAP (which stands for Supplemental Nutrition Assistance Program), helps people with low income buy the food they need for good health.

> **Wisconsin FoodShare (SNAP) Eligibility**
> - low-income employment
> - live on a small or fixed income
> - retired
> - have lost their job
> - disabled and cannot work

Cassie also has a half-brother named Nathan, who is four years older than her. When Becky died, Cassie hadn't seen Nathan in more than a year. Nathan, aged 26 when his mother passed away, needed assistance and direction from Lisa in managing Becky's funeral and burial. Both Nathan and Cassie struggled with conflicting feelings, having been abandoned by Becky at times and of course grief at the loss of their mother.

Cassie is now working with a social worker at her county's disability office on an application for social security disability benefits. The social worker also helped Cassie get assistance from a local community care agency. The agency assisted Lisa by calling her county's Aging and Disability Resource Center to speak first with an intake worker. The intake worker scheduled an interview for Lisa and Cassie with a social worker. The interview included a functional assessment to determine Cassie's eligibility for either Social Security Disability Insurance (SSDI) or the Children's long-term support (CLTS) Program. If eligible Cassie would then work with support and service coordinators under the CLTS program. The process also included Options Counseling to determine the best program, services, and information that would assist Cassie and her family to best meet her needs. If in this process the assessment determines that an application for disability is appropriate, the ADRC will then assist Cassie's family with the process. The process resulted in Cassie applying for SSDI; the application is currently pending. As was mentioned in Jay's journey, the disability application process is long and frustrating. A sizable percentage of applications are rejected on the first attempt. The information needed for a successful application includes extensive medical records and physician notes, work history (if applicable), scholastic records for young people, depending on age, and other factors.

One program that may be an option for Cassie after she gets her footing after a successful SSDI application and benefits, is to take part in the Medicaid Purchase Plan (MAPP). The program includes the ability to work substantially and create greater independence. It may be difficult to see that level of success and responsibility at this point, given Cassie's history, but time and forward movement and the stability of SSDI, coupled with MAPP, could be the level of support to make that happen. To make enrollment in MAPP most effective, disability benefits counseling will help Cassie to best use supports available. It is yet one more essential resource that can be accessed through the ADRC.

If Cassie were to have successful employment, she may reach substantial gainful activity (SGA) which could impact her SSDI benefit. SGA refers to the level of work activity that can affect eligibility for SSDI. SGA serves as a threshold to evaluate whether a person with a disability can engage in substantial work despite their condition. In 2026 the SGA limit is $1,690 /month, ($2,830) if the individual is blind. If an individual earns above this amount, they are generally considered to be engaging in SGA, which may disqualify them from receiving disability benefits. Benefits counseling can assist in helping Cassie determine the level of work effort and the implications upon her social security benefits.

When Cassie receives approval for social security disability based upon being legally blind, she will be eligible for services through the Wisconsin Office for the Blind and Visually Impaired (OBVI). Rehabilitation services are provided by OBVI to help individuals who are blind or visually impaired to achieve their own goals of independent living. OBVI staff visit individuals in their homes, conduct group training, and teach techniques and technologies for use in daily living (home management, personal care, orientation, mobility, and communications). These specialized skills allow individuals to adapt and adjust to vision loss, enabling them to live as independently as possible.

With Cassie now 22 years old, she will be in the adult system for disability if she gains approval. For families with younger children with autism seeking social security disability and other resources, I believe the following information would be helpful.

For children applying for disability, rather than looking at work factors, Social Security application reviewers assess whether a condition will cause severe functional limitations for at least a year or is likely to be fatal. Social Security's review of disability applications encompasses the 14 categories in the adult section plus one child-specific category: low birth weight and failure to thrive. The disability standard for minors is also different.

With the OBBBA passage discussed in the Medicaid chapter, work requirements under Medicaid and SNAP may impact Cassie. Will she be certified as medically or mentally exempt or will she be required to work or volunteer at the level of 20 hours per week to maintain her benefits eligibility? She can also seek to enroll in MAPP, Wisconsin's Medicaid buy-in program and utilize the available work incentives. This is one of many programs Cassie can seek to use by discussing them with her county ADRC and with the community care manager. Benefits counseling is another means that people with disabilities can use to assess how work may impact their Medicaid coverage and benefits eligibility. The ADRC can facilitate and recommend programs to assist Cassie.

Cassie's community care manager has also identified a unique opportunity for Cassie. While Cassie states she is not quite ready for it, she has the option to move into an apartment complex for adults with disabilities, but she was overwhelmed by it upon her first visit. The apartment is near Lisa's home, and Cassie is planning to move there in the coming months and start to increase her independence. Cassie is reapplying for disability benefits again as part of her overall effort toward achieving that independence.

It strikes me that many people in the mainstream of

society see those on Medicaid, SNAP, or other social supports as dependent on the welfare system. This is sad and a complete misrepresentation. Those of us who understand the safety net and know how it can truly work for those in need, the results are actually the exact opposite. Medicaid and other social supports actually lift people up and create opportunities for them to flourish. Medicaid and other social service supports are the thread that binds lives together and strengthens their resolve while knitting them into a community, rather than allowing the fabric to fray and tear. Medicaid coverage, SNAP benefits, and other resources and services fortify vulnerable individuals saving lives and extraordinary costs of uncompensated care upon our hospitals. By creating mechanisms for community care outside the institutional care of the past like the Southern Wisconsin Center, society gains from people with disabilities contributions such as work and volunteering.

Summary

Cassie's journey to self-determination and creating her best life has rounded a corner. The path now is clear. Cassie has come an enormous distance since that fateful day when a school social worker finally saw the neglect, fear, and hunger Cassie was facing back in 2017. That school social worker made a huge difference that day, creating an opportunity for change. It is Lisa who has continually been Cassie's guardian angel and lifeline. Lisa is the reason Cassie is on a positive path, having removed huge obstacles for Cassie. The future is unknown, but the path is now lighted by Lisa's care, advocacy, and love. Those three essential needs were missing in Cassie's life until Lisa entered it and created a pathway forward.

Book Summary

The coverage information and resources in this book provide a thorough overview of coverage and benefits offered for long-term care through Medicare, Medicaid, Veteran's and long-term care insurance. The most useful information and resources are available at county Aging and Disability Resource Centers, the Board on Aging and Long-term Care, the Board for People with Developmental Disabilities, and for those who live in Wisconsin, the Coalition of Wisconsin Aging Groups. For government program resources, these agency resources are also helpful: Centers for Medicare and Medicaid Services (www.cms.gov), Health care.gov, Wisconsin Department of Health Services (www.dhs.wisconsin.gov), or other state Medicaid health agencies. You can find additional resources, support, and assistance at my website: www.theltcresource. com and my podcast by the same name.

And finally, the four unique stories illustrate the difficult prospect of accessing and covering long-term care expenses and effective resources to navigate the complexity that comes with long-term care. There are numerous barriers faced by these individuals and their families, including benefit questions, disability eligibility, access to care, and more. Some barriers were successfully overcome, and others were challenging and seemed insurmountable. However, with the right information and assistance from caring people and available community resources, these challenges can be successfully navigated. It is my hope that I have supplied you with the resources and tools to help your loved ones gain access to the resources they need when they need them.

Appendix I: 2026 Federal Poverty Level (FPL) Guidelines:

The Federal Poverty Level (FPL) is an economic measure used to determine eligibility for various federal assistance programs, reflecting the minimum income needed for basic necessities. The Department of Health and Human Services (HHS) updates its poverty guidelines, illustrating the set minimum amount of income that a family needs for food, clothing, transportation, shelter, and other necessities, once a year, adjusted for inflation. The table below illustrates the income levels related to household size at various increments discussed within Part I and related to the 48 Contiguous States (all states except Alaska and Hawaii which are slightly higher) and (Figures below are in Dollars Per Year).

Family Size	100% FPL	133% FPL	138% FPL	200% FPL	300% FPL	400% FPL
1	$15,960	$21,227	$22,025	$31,920	$47,880	$63,840
2	$21,640	$28,781	$29,863	$43,280	$64,920	$86,560
3	$27,320	$36,336	$37,702	$54,640	$81,960	$109,280
4	$33,000	$43,890	$45,540	$66,000	$99,000	$132,000
5	$38,680	$51,444	$53,378	$77,360	$116,040	$154,720
6	$44,360	$58,988	$61,217	$88,720	$133,080	$177,440

Appendix II: Social Security Disability Application Part A and B Categories

As of this writing in November 2025, when adults apply for Social Security disability benefits, they are evaluated concerning their inability to engage in any substantial gainful activity (SGA) of employment by reason of any medically determinable physical or mental impairment(s). These impairments are deemed substantial and the disability benefit may be approved if the impairment can be expected to result in death or which has lasted or can be expected to last for a continuous period of not less than 12 months.

The Social Security Part A application, the adult section, is divided into 14 categories, representing types of disorders or diseases of various bodily systems:

1. Musculoskeletal system, such as amputation, chronic joint pain, and spinal disorders
2. Special senses and speech, such as impaired hearing, sight, or speech
3. Respiratory illnesses, such as asthma, chronic obstructive pulmonary disease (COPD), and cystic fibrosis
4. Cardiovascular illnesses, such as arrhythmia, congenital heart disease, and heart failure
5. Digestive system, such as bowel or liver disease
6. Chronic kidney disease
7. Blood disorders, such as sickle cell disease and other anemias, bone marrow failure, or hemophilia
8. Skin disorders, such as burns, dermatitis, and ichthyosis, a group of about 20 conditions that cause dryness and scaling

9. Endocrine disorders, such as diabetes and thyroid problems

10. Congenital disorders such as Down syndrome that affect multiple body systems

11. Neurological disorders, such as amyotrophic lateral sclerosis (ALS), epilepsy, multiple sclerosis, Parkinson's disease, and traumatic brain injuries

12. Cognitive and mental health conditions, such as bipolar disorder, dementia, depression, intellectual disabilities, and schizophrenia

13. Cancer

14. Immune system diseases, such as human immunodeficiency virus (HIV), inflammatory arthritis, and lupus

The Social Security Part B application, the childhood listings as of November 2025, encompass the 14 categories in the adult section plus one child-specific category, related to an infant's low birth weight and failure to thrive. A child under age 18 is approved for disability benefits if he or she has a medically determinable physical or mental impairment or combination of impairments that causes marked and severe functional limitations. Furthermore, that impairment or combination of impairments is disabling for a child if it can be expected to cause death or that has lasted or can be expected to last for a continuous period of not less than 12 months.

References:

1. "Health care Spending as a Percentage of GDP by Country, 2023," Statista, Statista website, accessed 7/1/2025
2. US Health Expenditure as GDP Share data, 1960-2022, Statista, by Preeti Vankar, February 16, 2024
3. "What the Data Says About Medicaid," Pew Research Center, by Drew Desilver, 6/24/25, www.pewresearch.org/short-reads/2025/06/24/what-the-data-says-about-medicaid
4. "US Health Care System Ranks Last Overall Among Other High-Income Countries," American Journal of Managed Care, by Pearl Steinzor, September 19, 2024, www.ajmc.com%2fview%2fus-health-care-system-ranks-last-overall-among-other-high-income-countries
5. "Philanthropy at Work Reports," John A Hartford Foundation: October 2024,
6. Posted October 17, 2024, https://www.gih.org/philanthropy-work/reports/john-a-hartford-foundation-october-2024/
7. "Warning From Older Adults: Care for Aging in America Needs Urgent Rethinking," The John Hartford Foundation, 9/17/2024, https://www.johnahartford.org/newsroom/view/warning-from-older-adults-care-for-aging-in-america-needs-urgent-rethinking
8. "The State of Health Insurance Coverage in the US," 11/21/2024, Commonwealth Fund, https://www.commonwealthfund.org/publications/surveys/2024/nov/state-health-insurance-coverage-us-2024-biennial-survey
9. "What is Long-Term Care Insurance," Forbes Magazine,

by Elaine Shelly, 5/16/2024, https://www.forbes.com/
health/senior-living/long-term-care-insurance/

10. "Long-term Care Statistics 2025" Consumer Affairs
Journal, 2/6/2024, www.consumeraffairs.com/health/
long-term-care-statistics.html

11. "Long-term care needs will only increase as more
americans age," by Susan Rupe, 12/4/24, https://
insurancenewsnet.com/innarticle/long-term-care-
needs-will-only-increase-as-more-americans-age

12. "Are partnerships the answer to the long-term
care crisis?," Insurance News Net, 12/11/24, https://
insurancenewsnet.com/innarticle/are-partnerships-the-
answer-to-the-long-term-care-crisis

13. "One in Five 5 Americans Now Provide Unpaid
Family Care," by Deborah Schoch 7/15/2022, https://
www.aarp.org/caregiving/basics/info-2020/unpaid-
family-caregivers-report.html

14. "Employer health care spending in 2025: Why it's
likely to accelerate," by Yulan Egan, Union Health care
Insight, https://www.unionhealth careinsight.com/
post/why-employer-health care-spending-in-2025-is-
expected-to-accelerate

15. "Disability insurance demystified: Choosing between
short-term and long-term coverage," Jon Davis, Onpay
website, 4/8/25, https://onpay.com/insights/disability-
insurance-short-term-vs-long-term-benefits

16. "Final Regulations Address ACA Exchange Integrity;
Revise 2026 Annual Limitation on Cost-Sharing,"
6/25/2025. Thomson Reuters website, https://tax.
thomsonreuters.com/news/final-regulations-address-
aca-exchange-integrity-revise-2026-annual-limitation-
on-cost-sharing/

17. "Affordable Care Act Has Narrowed Racial and

Ethnic Gaps in Access to Health Care, But Progress Has Stalled," Commonwealth Fund, 1/16/2020, https://www.commonwealthfund.org/press-release/2020/new-report-affordable-care-act-has-narrowed-racial-and-ethnic-gaps-access-health

18. "Eliminating the Medicaid Expansion Federal Match Rate: State-by-State Estimates," Kaiser Family Foundation, by Elizabeth Williams, Alice Burns, Rhiannon Euhus, and Robin Rudowitz, 2/13/2025, https://www.kff.org /medicaid/issue-brief/eliminating-the-medicaid-expansion-federal-match-rate-state-by-state-estimates/

19. "The State of Health Insurance Coverage in the US: Findings from the Commonwealth Fund 2024 Biennial Health Insurance Survey," Sara R. Collins and Avni Gupta, (Commonwealth Fund, Nov. 2024). https://doi.org/10.26099/byce-qc28

20. "Health Insurance Coverage: Early Release of Estimates from the National Health Interview Survey, 2010," Robin A. Cohen, Brian W. Ward, and Jeannine S. Schiller, (Centers for Disease Control and Prevention, National Center for Health Statistics, June 2011)

21. "A Closer Look at the Remaining Uninsured Population Eligible for Medicaid and CHIP," Kaiser Family Foundation, March 2024. Accessed at: A Closer Look at the Remaining Uninsured Population Eligible for Medicaid and CHIP.

22. Ibid

23. "Eliminating the Medicaid Expansion Federal Match Rate: State-by-State Estimates," by Elizabeth Williams, Alice Burns, Rhiannon Euhus, and Robin Rudowitz, 2/13/2025, https://www.kff.org/medicaid/issue-brief/

eliminating-the-medicaid-expansion-federal-match-rate-state-by-state-estimates/

24. "How the American Rescue Plan Will Improve Affordability of Private Health Insurance," Kaiser Family Foundation," by Karen Pollitz, 3/17/21, https://www.kff.org/affordable-care-act/issue-brief/how-the-american-rescue-plan-will-improve-affordability-of-private-health-coverage/

25. "How the ACA Health Insurance Subsidy Works," Very Well Health, 10/15/2023, https://www.verywellhealth.com/how-the-health-insurance-subsidy-works-1738915

26. "Record number of Americans enroll in ACA," Insurance News Net, January, 22, 2025, https://insurancenewsnet.com/article/record-number-of-americans-enroll-in-aca

27. "Marketplace 2025 Open Enrollment Period Report: National Snapshot," Center for Medicare and Medicaid Services website, accessed 6/29/25, https://www.cms.gov/newsroom/fact-sheets/marketplace-2025-open-enrollment-period-report-national-snapshot-2

28. "Trump Administration Proposes ObamaCare Enrollment Changes," Kaiser Family Foundation Health News, Julie Appleby, 3/11/2025, https://www.usnews.com/news/health-news/articles/2025-03-11/trump-administration-proposes-obamacare-enrollment-changes

29. "January 2025: Medicaid and CHIP Eligibility Operations and Enrollment Snapshot, Medicaid.gov website, https://www.medicaid.gov/resources-for-states/downloads/eligib-oper-and-enrol-snap-january2025.pdf

30. "The Implications of Federal SNAP Spending Cuts on

Individuals with Medicaid, Medicare and Other Health Coverage," 6/26/2025, Kaiser Family Foundation, by Aubrey Winger, Nancy Ochieng, Akash Pillai, Matthew Rae, Juliette Cubanski, Emma Wager, and Robin Rudowitz, https://www.kff.org/medicaid/issue-brief/the-implications-of-federal-snap-spending-cuts-on-individuals-with-medicaid-and-other-health-coverage/

31. "State News, Congress Pushing for a Medicaid Work Requirement. Here's What Happened when Georgia tried it," Mostly Medicaid webpage, accessed 7/7/2025, https://mostlymedicaid.com/state-news-congress-is-pushing-for-a-medicaid-work-requirement-heres-what-happened-when-Georgia-tried-it/?mc_cid=e1391151b&mc_eid=5c9edc2b28

32. "Here's When Each Part of Trump's 'Big, Beautiful Bill' takes Effect," MSN, by Aliss Higham, https://www.msn.com/en-us/news/politics/heres-when-each-part-of-trumps-big-beautiful-bill-takes-effect/ar-AA1HYVLy?ocid=BingNewsSerp

33. "Understanding the Intersection of Medicaid and Work: An Update," Kaiser Family Foundation, by Jennifer Tolbert, Sammy Cervantes, Robin Rudowitz, and Alice Burns, 5/30/2025, https://www.kff.org/medicaid/issue-brief/understanding-the-intersection-of-medicaid-and-work-an-update/

34. "2024 Medicaid & CHIP Beneficiaries at a Glance: Maternal Health," Medicaid.gov website, May 2024, https://www.medicaid.gov/medicaid/benefits/downloads/2024-maternal-health-at-a-glance.pdf

35. "Does Medicaid Cover Nearly Half of all Births in the US," GigaFact by Eric Gretzinger of Wisconsin Watch, 3/11/23, https://gigafact.org/fact-briefs/does-medicaid-cover-nearly-half-of-all-births-in-the-us/

36. "The State of Children with Disabilities and Special Health Care Needs," By the Annie E. Casey Foundation, 7/14/24

37. "Children with Special Health Care Needs: Coverage, Affordability, and HCBS Access," Kaiser Family Foundation, 10/4/21, https://www.kff.org/medicaid/issue-brief/children-with-special-health-care-needs-coverage-affordability-and-hcbs-access/

38. "5 Key Facts About Children with Special Health Care Needs and Medicaid," Elizabeth Williams, Kaiser Family Foundation, 4/18/2025, https://www.kff.org/medicaid/issue-brief/5-key-facts-about-children-with-special-health-care-needs-and-medicaid/

39. "Medicaid Renewal Data," Wisconsin Department of Health Services, website accessed 7/5/2025, https://www.dhs.wisconsin.gov/medicaid/renewal-data.htm

40. "5 Key Facts About Children with Special Health Care Needs and Medicaid," Elizabeth Williams, Kaiser Family Foundation, 4/18/2025, https://www.kff.org/medicaid/issue-brief/5-key-facts-about-children-with-special-health-care-needs-and-medicaid/

41. Children and Youth with Special Health Care Needs webpage, Wisconsin Department of Health Services, accessed 7/5/2025, https://www.dhs.wisconsin.gov/cyshcn/index.htm

42. "Symptoms of the Crisis," For Others, Accessed 4/14/25, https://www.forothers.com/the-crisis/?msclkid=6feea409bb751cb9c60dc3f453628324&utm_source=bing&utm_medium=cpc&utm_campaign=FO%20-%20Crisis%20And%20Solution&utm_term=how%20many%20children%20are%20in%20foster%20care&utm_

content=Number%20Of%20Children%20In%20
Foster%20Care

43. US Department of Health & Human Services,
Administration for Children and Families,
Administration on Children, Youth and Families,
Children's Bureau. (2024). Child Maltreatment FY2023.
Available here https://www.acf.hhs.gov/cb/data-
research/child-maltreatment.

44. US Department of Health and Human Services,
Administration for Children and Families,
Administration on Children, Youth and Families,
Children's Bureau, "The AFCARS Report," (2024),
Available here https://acf.gov/cb/report/afcars-
report-30

45. E. Stoltzfus et al. "Child Welfare: Health Care Needs
of Children in Foster Care and Related Federal Issues,"
US Congressional Research Service (November, 2014).
Available here https://sgp.fas.org/crs/misc/R42378.pdf

46. "US Adoption and Foster Care Statistics,"
Congressional Coalition on Adoption Institute website
Accessed 7/5/2025, https://www.ccainstitute.org/
resources/fact-sheets#:~:text=46%25%20of%20the%20
children%20and%20youth%20who%20left,and%20
other%20environments%2C%20instead%20of%20
with%20a%20family.

47. "1 in 31 US Kids has Autism, CDC says," by Erika
Edwards, Today.com, 4/15/25, https://www.today.com/
parents/family/autism-rate-increases-cdc-rcna201436

48. Ibid.

49. "Major changes could be coming to BadgerCare Plus,
Medicaid in Wisconsin. Here's what to know," Laura
Schulte, Sarah Volpenhein, and Lawrence Andrea,
Milwaukee Journal Sentinel, 5/22/2025

50. "Policy Brief on Medicaid & CHIP: Recommendations to Assist Youth and Young Adults with Disabilities Aging Out of Medicaid & CHIP," The National Alliance to Advance Adolescent Health/ Got Transition, July, 2024, https://gottransition.org/ resource/?policy-brief-medicaid-chip

51. ibid.

52. "Too Many Babies Miss Out on Medicaid Infant Coverage, Promising Practices Point the Way for States," by Kay Johnson, Georgetown University Center for Children and Families, 3/10/2021, https://ccf. georgetown.edu/2021/03/10/too-many-babies-miss-out-on-medicaid-infant-coverage/

53. "Why doesn't America's health care system work for older people?" by Richard Eisenberg, 10/12/2024, Morningstar," https://www.morningstar.com/news/ marketwatch/20241012265/why-doesnt-americas-health care-system-work-for-older-people

54. "March 2023 Medicaid and CHIP Enrollment Data Highlights," July 2023, Centers for Medicare and Medicaid Services, https://www.medicaid.gov/ medicaid/program-information/medicaid-and-chip-enrollment-data/report-highlights/index.html

55. "Older People Projected to Outnumber Children for first time in US History," United States Census Bureau, March 13, 2018, https://www.census.gov/newsroom/ press-releases/2018/cb18-41-population-projections. html

56. "Medicare Advantage 2025 Spotlight: A First Look at Plan Offerings," Kaiser Family Foundation, Meredith Freed, Jeannie Fuglesten Biniek, Anthony Damico, and Tricia Neuman, 11/15/2024, https://www.kff.

org/medicare/issue-brief/medicare-advantage-2025-spotlight-a-first-look-at-plan-offerings/

57. Ibid.

58. "Traditional Medicare or Medicare Advantage: How Older Americans Choose and Why," The Commonwealth Fund, by Faith Leonard, Gretchen Jacobson, Lauren A. Haynes, Sara R. Collins, 10/17/2022, https://www.commonwealthfund.org/publications/issue-briefs/2022/oct/traditional-medicare-or-advantage-how-older-americans-choose

59. "The Economics of Medicare Advantage vs Medicare Supplement Enrollment," eHealth Insurance, March, 2023,

60. https://news.ehealthinsurance.com/_ir/68/20232/eHealth_Economics_Medicare_Advantage_Medicare_Supplement_Enrollment_March2023.pdf#:~:text=By%20contrast%2C%20Medicare%20Supplement%20enrollees%20worry%20most%20about,being%20unable%20to%20afford%20their%20medical%20care%20%2827%25%29.

61. "Who Are the Nation's Veterans," USA Facts, 4/14/2025, https://usafacts.org/articles/who-are-the-nations-veterans/

62. "Dementia Care in Wisconsin," Department of Health Services website, 5/7/25, https://www.dhs.wisconsin.gov/dementia/index.htm

63. "Genworth and CareScout Release Cost of Care Survey Results for 2024," by Ryan Clark, 3/4/2025, https://investor.genworth.com/news-events/press-releases/detail/982/genworth-and-carescout-release-cost-of-care-survey-results

64. "HHS Layoffs hot Meals on Wheels and other

Services for Seniors and Disabled," National Public Radio, by Joseph Shapiro, 4/1/2025

65. "Why Falls Can Turn Deadly as You Age," AARP website, by Rachel Nania, 6/19/2025, https://www.aarp.org/health/conditions-treatments/deadly-falls/?msockid=1e9b83e4ca3063d9196b900ecb7f6242

66. Ibid.

67. "The Silent Epidemic of Senior Loneliness," Honor Care, By Seth Sternberg, 4/29/2025   https://www.honorcare.com/news/silent-epidemic-of-senior-loneliness/

68. PIRATE Program description, Veterans Health Foundation, Pittsburgh, PA, https://veteranshealthfoundation.org/pirate/, website accessed 5/2/2025

About the Author

Michael Meulemans is a recognized expert on Medicaid, Medicare, the Affordable Care Act, and long-term care coverage and resources. He has over 25 years' experience in Medicaid policy specializing in long-term services and supports and Medicaid managed care services for the aged and people with disabilities. In addition, he has managed the sale of Medicare health plans and was a consultant involved in Affordable Care Act health plan implementation. Past publications include insurance continuing education textbooks written for America's Health Insurance Plans' continuing education program on the following topics: Fundamentals of Health Insurance, Supplemental Health Insurance, and others. He serves on the board of directors of the Wisconsin Alzheimer's Association and a local long-term care services provider, Community Living Alliance. He resides in Madison, WI. You can reach him at mjm@theltcresource.com and visit www.theLTCResource.com where you can find a link to the LTC Resource Podcast or subscribe on Spotify/ Buzzsprout.

If you thought this book was helpful, please help others find the book by leaving a review on your favorite book website. Reviews are extremely helpful for indie-authors like Michael.

~ Thank you